MY FIRST

ATLAS

Katie John Sharp

Consultant:

Phil Klein, Ph.D.

Publications International, Ltd.

Writer:
Katie John Sharp is a children's book author and editor. She contributed to World Book's *World Adventure* series and has written for numerous other children's publishers, including Rigby Education, Heinemann Library, and Brown Publishing Network.

Consultant:
Phil Klein, Ph.D., is associate professor of geography at the University of Northern Colorado. He has written several publications in geography education, including instructional materials for both elementary and secondary schools. He is a member of the Association of American Geographers and the National Council for Geographic Education.

Louis Weber, CEO
Publications International, Ltd.
7373 North Cicero Avenue
Lincolnwood, Illinois 60712

www.myactiveminds.com

Permission is never granted for commercial purposes.

ActiveMinds® is a registered trademark of Publications International, Ltd.

Printed in Hong Kong.

8 7 6 5 4 3 2 1

ISBN-13: 978-0-7853-8371-0
ISBN-10: 0-7853-8371-9

Library of Congress Control Number: 2003109991

Contents

Reading Maps

An atlas is a book of maps. Maps show you where things are. They display what the world looks like and where you can find things like continents, oceans, countries, cities, lakes, islands, rivers, and mountains.

This atlas has a map of every country in the world. It also has pictures and more information about those countries and regions. This page explains some of the features you can find on a map of the world.

The **equator** is an imaginary line that circles the earth right in the middle. It divides the earth into the Northern Hemisphere and the Southern Hemisphere.

The tropics are regions on either side of the equator. Locations around the tropics are very hot year-round because the sun always shines almost directly overhead. The **Tropic of Cancer** is an imaginary line that marks the tropics' northern boundary. The **Tropic of Capricorn** is an imaginary line that marks their southern boundary.

Latitude and **longitude** help you to find a location on the earth. Most maps are marked with a system of lines. The lines that go in an east-west direction are called lines of latitude. They tell you how far north or south from the equator a place is. The lines that go in a north-south direction are called lines of longitude. They tell you how far east or west a place is from the Prime Meridian, which runs through Western Europe and West Africa. They run from the North Pole to the South Pole. Latitude and longitude are measured in degrees.

The **Antarctic Circle** is an imaginary line that goes through parts of Antarctica. At every point south of this line, there is at least one day in every year when the sun does not set and another when it does not rise.

150° W   120° W   90° W

75° N

ARCTIC CIRCLE

60° N

NORTH AMERICA

30° N

TROPIC OF CANCER

0°   EQUATOR

SOUTH AMERICA

TROPIC OF CAPRICORN

30° S

60° S

ANTARCTIC CIRCLE

75° S

150° W   120° W   90° W

4

The **Arctic Circle** is an imaginary line that runs through the northern parts of Canada, Alaska, Russia, Scandinavia, and Greenland. At every point north of this line, there is at least one day in every year when the sun does not set and another when it does not rise.

The **North Pole** is in the middle of the Arctic Ocean. It is the most northern point on the earth.

A **compass rose** shows you the direction of north (N) on a map. Sometimes it also shows you the directions of south (S), east (E), and west (W). You can use the points of a compass to describe where a place is located. For example, Europe is north of Africa and west of Asia. Asia is both north and west of Australia, so you can use a combination of compass points and say that Asia is northwest (NW) of Australia.

30° W 0° 30° E 60° E 90° E 120° E 150° E 180° E

75° N

ARCTIC CIRCLE

60° N

EUROPE   ASIA

30° N

TROPIC OF CANCER

AFRICA

PRIME MERIDIAN

EQUATOR   0°

TROPIC OF CAPRICORN

AUSTRALIA

30° S

60° S

ANTARCTIC CIRCLE

75° S

ANTARCTICA

30° W 0° 30° E 60° E 90° E 120° E 150° E 180° E

0 500 1000 1500 miles

The **South Pole** is located in Antarctica. It is the most southern point on the earth.

The **scale** shows you how the distance on a map compares with the real distance on the ground. For example, one inch on the map may represent five miles on the ground. Many scales are shown as a bar divided into sections or units. In the scale shown on this map, each section or unit of the bar is equal to 500 miles. Scales change from map to map, depending on the size of the area a map shows.

5

World Continents

The land in the world is divided into seven large masses called continents and thousands of smaller masses called islands. Asia is the largest continent, followed by Africa, North America, South America, Antarctica, Europe, and Australia. More than half of the world's people live in Asia, while no one makes a permanent home in Antarctica.

North America stretches from the frozen Arctic Ocean to the beautiful tropical shores of the Caribbean Sea. It includes the countries of Canada, the United States, and Mexico, as well as the countries in Central America, the island of Greenland, and the islands of the Caribbean Sea.

ARCTIC OCEAN

NORTH AMERICA

ATLANTIC OCEAN

PACIFIC OCEAN

South America is almost completely surrounded by water. The Caribbean Sea lies to the north, the Atlantic Ocean to the east, and the Pacific Ocean to the west. South America has 13 countries. The world's largest tropical rain forest grows in the Amazon River Basin, which covers about one-third of the continent.

SOUTH AMERICA

Population Density
Number of people per square mile

☐ Not Populated
☐ 0–65 persons/square mile
▨ 65–500
▨ 500–1,000
▨ 1,000–2,000
■ more than 2,000

Antarctica is an ice-covered continent that surrounds the South Pole. It is the only continent that does not have countries. The freezing cold waters of the Atlantic, Indian, and Pacific Oceans separate Antarctica from the other continents. Antarctica has no permanent population.

Just over six billion people live on the earth. You are one of them! This population is not spread evenly over the continents. Few people live in deserts or polar regions, where food and water are hard to find and the temperatures are unbearable. So, where are all the people? They live in fertile areas, where the soil is rich for farming and raising animals. They live close to energy sources, such as oil, where they can use the energy to run machinery or heat their homes. They often live near rivers and ocean coasts so they have a good water supply or can transport goods into and out of their land. Almost half the world's people live in cities. On this map, places with the most people are shown in red. Places with the least people are shown in white.

Europe has 44 countries. Russia, which lies partly in Europe and partly in Asia, is the largest, and Vatican City is the smallest. Europe stretches from the Arctic Ocean in the north to the Mediterranean Sea in the south, and from the Atlantic Ocean in the west to the Ural Mountains in the east.

Asia is the largest continent and has the most people. It stretches from Africa and Europe in the west to the Pacific Ocean in the east. The northern part of Asia lies within the frozen Arctic Circle. In the south near the equator, Asia has steaming hot tropics. The continent is divided into 48 countries, plus other political units.

EUROPE

ASIA

AFRICA

INDIAN OCEAN

Africa is the second-largest continent in both area and population. It lies between the Atlantic and Indian Oceans. Africa is divided into 53 independent countries and several other political units. Much of northern Africa is covered by the world's largest desert, the Sahara. Africa also has the world's longest river—the Nile.

AUSTRALIA

Australia is the smallest continent. It is so small that some people call it "the island continent." Only one country, Australia, is on this continent.

SOUTHERN OCEAN

ANTARCTICA

Climates and Landforms

What is the climate in your part of the world? Is it hot or cold? Is it mostly wet or dry? Does it snow or rain? Or do you get a little bit of everything? The conditions around you, such as the temperature and rainfall, make up your region's climate. An area's climate depends partly on how far it is from the equator. Usually, regions near the equator are the hottest places, while those near the North or South Poles are the coldest. Land near the sea usually gets more rainfall and has a steadier temperature year-round than areas away from the sea. Cooler temperatures are more normal on higher land than on low-lying areas. Here are some different climates found around the world.

Look out your window. Do you see towering mountains capped with snow? Or do you see rolling hills that climb up and down like a roller coaster? Maybe there is flat land that stretches as far as you can see.

The earth is covered with these three landforms—plains, mountains, or hills. And the land continually changes—but so slowly that you do not notice it. Every place on the earth has its own landform. Some even have more than one!

Boreal forests have long, cold winters and short summers. Evergreen forests cover these areas. Northern Canada, Iceland, Siberia, and parts of Norway, Sweden, and Finland have boreal forests, as do parts of Chile and New Zealand.

Temperate forests cover many parts of North America, South America, Europe, and northern Asia. These areas have regular rainfall. Temperatures never climb very high or fall very low. Some trees that rise in these forests grow new leaves each spring. The leaves change color and fall off each autumn.

Plains are large areas of flat land. They are sometimes covered with grass, low shrubs, and few trees. Plains may be found along an ocean or inland.

Hills are low, raised landforms that are often rounded on top. They are higher than plains but not nearly as high as mountains.

Mountains are large masses of earth and rock that rise above the surrounding land. They are usually much higher than hills. The higher you climb a mountain, the colder the air becomes. Above a certain height, called the tree line, it becomes too cold even for trees to grow. Did you know that even the oceans have mountains? Mauna Kea is a volcano on the island of Hawaii in North America. Its rise from base on the ocean floor to peak is the greatest in the world.

The **tundra and ice caps** are areas where it is very cold in winter, and the summers are short. Temperatures here rarely rise above freezing. The North and South Poles are covered in ice hundreds of feet thick. Land near the Poles is covered with cold, dry plains, where few plants can grow. These areas are called tundra.

Grasslands and **shrublands** experience extreme heat and sometimes extreme cold. The rich soil of grasslands and shrublands makes them ideal for growing crops. Different kinds of grasses and shrubs grow on this land, providing food for grazing animals. The North American prairies and the Russian steppes are examples of grasslands. They can also be found in Africa and South America. In tropical areas, grasslands are sometimes called savannas.

Deserts often lie near the tropics. They receive little or no rainfall. Parts of the Sahara, the Australian Outback, and Chile's Atacama Desert can go for years without any rain. Only plants and animals that have adapted to life in the desert can survive these harsh environments.

Tropical forests are low-lying regions around the equator that are hot and wet throughout the year. Thick rain forests cover these regions. They are home to the world's greatest variety of plant and animal life. Tropical forests are found in South America, Africa, and Asia.

World Land Use

Think of all the things you use every day that come from the earth. You take a bath in water that comes from rivers and lakes. You drink milk from cows raised on farms. You eat cereal made from grains grown on farmland. Your kitchen table is made from the wood of trees. You ride a car or bus, which runs on gasoline from oil. All of these products come from the earth.

Long ago, people worked the land to grow food just for their families or communities. They used natural products to build their homes and to make clothing. In many parts of the world, this is still the case. In other areas, however, people work to get earth's products to other homes, other cities, and other countries. This is called economic activity. Here are some basic ways in which people can use the land for economic activity.

Forestry, the business of growing, caring for, and harvesting forest trees, is a very old economic activity. People have relied on the trees that grow in forests for thousands of years. Forest products provide people with food, shelter, clothing, and fuel.

Predominant economy
- Agriculture
- Agriculture and forestry
- Fishing
- Forestry (lumber and pulpwood)
- Hunting, fishing, and forestry
- Subsistence agriculture
- Little or no economic activity
- Manufacturing
- Nomadic herding
- Stock raising on ranges

In **subsistence farming,** farmers grow just enough food to meet their own needs. They grow food for their families and maybe a little bit more for their communities. They do not have any left over to sell to others. Subsistence farming involves a lot of hard work and only basic farm tools. Millions of farmers in Africa, Asia, and Central America are subsistence farmers.

Many people raise animals for a living, which is called **livestock ranching** or **grazing.** Livestock are animals raised to produce food and other products. People eat the meat and drink the milk of these animals. Unlike nomadic herders, ranchers sell their products to others. The main kinds of livestock raised throughout the world are cattle, hogs, chickens, sheep, and horses. The skins of some livestock provide important materials, such as leather and wool. The organs of some livestock are used to make drugs that help treat sick people. Grassland areas are good for raising livestock.

Crop farming is the most important economic activity in the world. People cannot live without food, and nearly all the food we eat comes from crops grown on farms. Crop farmers grow plants to sell for food or manufacture. Crops for manufacture include wheat for flour, cotton for fabrics, or corn for feeding livestock. People most easily grow food on plains or in river valleys, where the soil is rich and deep. Rice is the world's most important crop, feeding half the world's population. It normally grows in warm, wet climates.

Manufacturing is the business of making new products from both raw materials and recycled materials. Raw materials are natural products used to make new products. Recycled materials, such as glass, metal, plastic, and paper, are reused to make new products. If you look around, you will see all kinds of manufactured goods. They include the television you watch, the furniture you sit on, the clothes you wear, the pencil you write with, and even this book! Europe produces more manufactured goods than any other continent. Most manufacturing activity takes place in major cities.

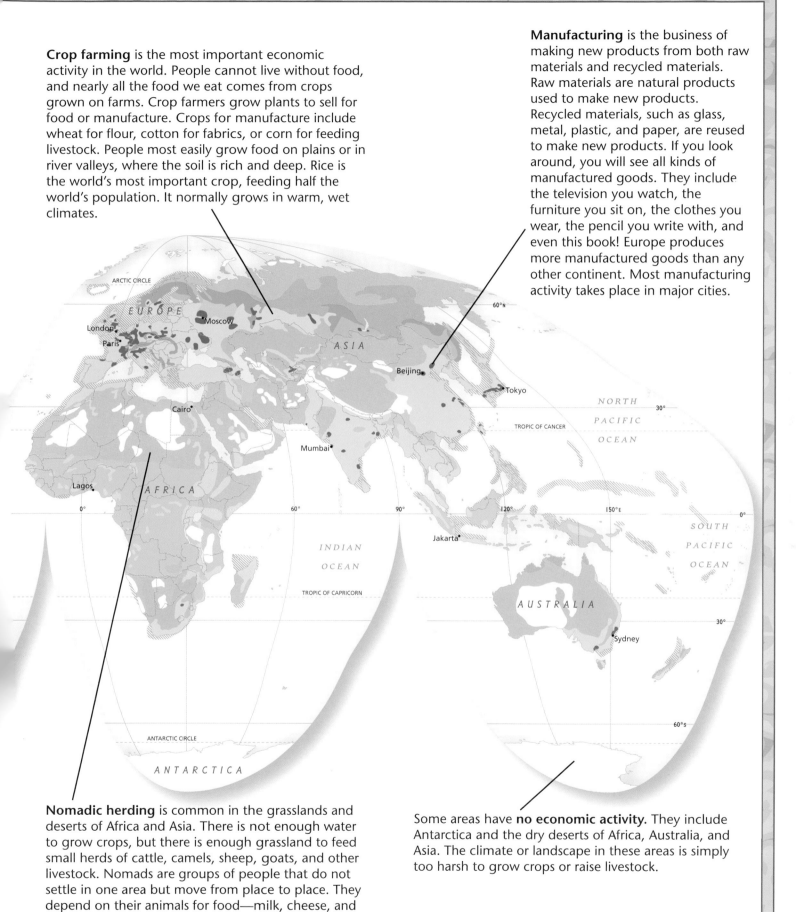

ARCTIC CIRCLE

EUROPE
London
Paris
Moscow
ASIA
Beijing
Tokyo
Cairo
60°N
NORTH PACIFIC OCEAN
30°
TROPIC OF CANCER
Mumbai
AFRICA
Lagos
0°
60°
90°
120°
150°E
0°
Jakarta
INDIAN OCEAN
SOUTH PACIFIC OCEAN
TROPIC OF CAPRICORN
AUSTRALIA
30°
Sydney
60°S
ANTARCTIC CIRCLE
ANTARCTICA

Nomadic herding is common in the grasslands and deserts of Africa and Asia. There is not enough water to grow crops, but there is enough grassland to feed small herds of cattle, camels, sheep, goats, and other livestock. Nomads are groups of people that do not settle in one area but move from place to place. They depend on their animals for food—milk, cheese, and meat. Nomads live in tents and wear clothing made from the skins and hair of their animals.

Some areas have **no economic activity.** They include Antarctica and the dry deserts of Africa, Australia, and Asia. The climate or landscape in these areas is simply too harsh to grow crops or raise livestock.

North America

North America is the third-largest continent in area. Only Asia and Africa have more land. North America stretches from the Arctic Ocean to South America. It has the fourth-largest population of all the continents.

North America is home to 23 countries, including Canada, the United States, and Mexico. The climate and landforms here offer a little bit of everything. There are frozen ice caps and tropical forests, magnificent mountains and flat grasslands, lush forests and hot, dry deserts. North America includes some of the world's biggest cities, but it is also home to wide-open areas of complete wilderness.

Most North Americans have their roots in Europe. Many Europeans came to North America a long time ago to live a new life. Today, their children, grandchildren, great-grandchildren, and more generations make up much of the varied population here. There are also many people of African origin and Asian origin living in North America. And finally, there are the native peoples. They lived here long before anyone else came to this land to explore.

Some European countries, such as the United Kingdom and France, have territory here. Greenland, for instance, belongs to Denmark.

U.S.A.

UNITED
OF A

NORTH

PACIFIC

OCEAN

MEXIC

U.S.A.

0   500   1000   1500 miles

ARCTIC OCEAN

GREENLAND

(DENMARK)

CANADA

ATES

RICA

NORTH

ATLANTIC

OCEAN

THE BAHAMAS

CUBA

DOMINICAN
REP.

HAITI

BELIZE   JAMAICA

SAINT KITTS AND NEVIS   ANTIGUA AND BARBUDA

EMALA   HONDURAS

DOMINICA
SAINT LUCIA
SAINT VINCENT AND THE GRENADINES   BARBADOS
GRENADA

EL
VADOR   NICARAGUA

TRINIDAD
AND TOBAGO

COSTA RICA

PANAMA

SOUTH AMERICA

Highest point: Mount McKinley (Alaska), 20,320 feet
Lowest point: Death Valley (California), 282 feet below sea level
Major rivers: Mackenzie (Canada), 2,635 miles; Missouri (United States), 2,540 miles; Mississippi (United States), 2,340 miles
Biggest lakes: Superior (United States, Canada), 31,700 square miles; Huron (United States, Canada), 23,000 square miles; Michigan (United States), 22,300 square miles
Major mountains: Mount McKinley (Alaska), 20,320 feet; Mount Logan (Canada), 19,550 feet; Volcan Pico de Orizaba (Mexico), 18,700 feet
Total land area: 8,300,000 square miles
Total population: 500,000,000
Largest country (area): Canada (3,851,810 square miles)
Smallest country (area): Saint Kitts and Nevis (101 square miles)
Largest country (population): United States (290,350,000)
Smallest country (population): Saint Kitts and Nevis (40,000)

13

United States

The United States is made up of 50 different states. It sits in the middle of North America, stretching from the Atlantic Ocean in the east to the Pacific Ocean in the west. It also includes two very different land areas, Alaska and Hawaii. Alaska is located in the northwest corner of North America. Hawaii is far out in the Pacific Ocean. The United States of America is the third-largest country in the world in population and in area.

The United States is a land of great diversity. People from every continent have moved here. Most of them brought their ways of life with them.

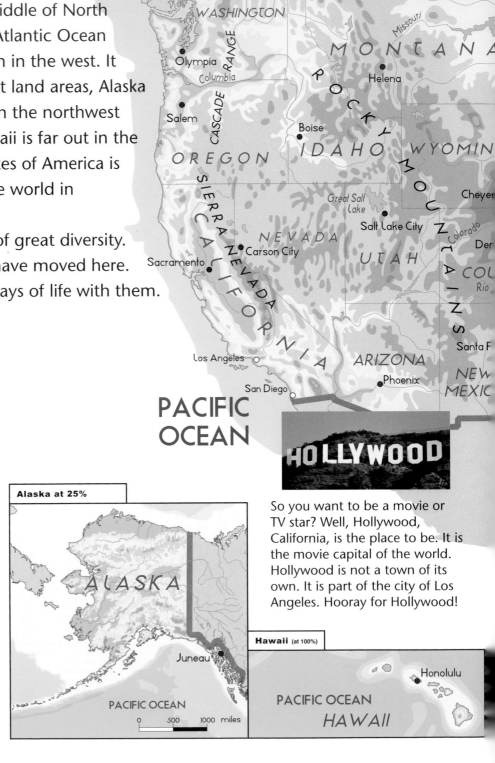

PACIFIC OCEAN

Alaska at 25%

PACIFIC OCEAN

0   500   1000 miles

Hawaii (at 100%)

PACIFIC OCEAN
HAWAII

So you want to be a movie or TV star? Well, Hollywood, California, is the place to be. It is the movie capital of the world. Hollywood is not a town of its own. It is part of the city of Los Angeles. Hooray for Hollywood!

Meaning of the Stars and Stripes

Look at the flag of the United States. What do you notice about it? First, you may see that it is red, white, and blue. Second, you notice that it has both stars and stripes. The flag has 13 stripes. There are seven red stripes and six white stripes. The stripes stand for the first 13 states of the country. The 50 white stars count the current number of states.

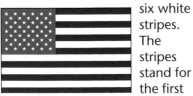

Some people call the American flag the Stars and Stripes. The Stars and Stripes stand for the land, the people, the government, and the ideals of the United States.

The bald eagle is the national bird of the United States. It is found only in North America. For a time, these birds were in danger of becoming extinct. People have worked hard to save them. Happily, more and more bald eagles are flying the skies again.

Thanksgiving is celebrated in the United States in November. It is a holiday for giving thanks and being with family. Turkey is a favorite food on Thanksgiving. According to legend, the Pilgrims and Native Americans served turkey at the first Thanksgiving. They gave thanks for the crops that grew that year.

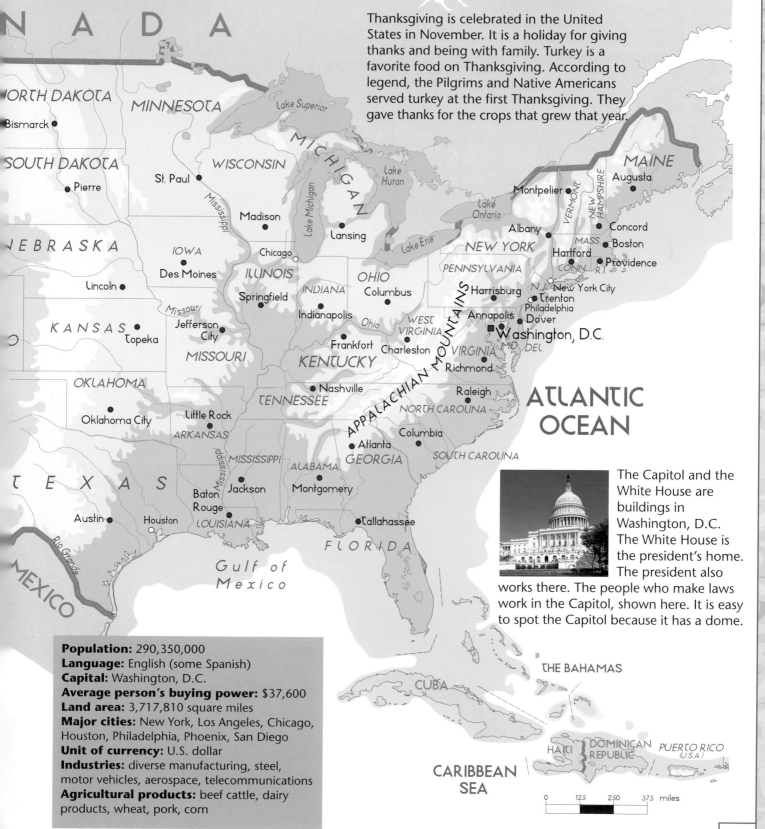

CANADA

NORTH DAKOTA
Bismarck

SOUTH DAKOTA
Pierre

NEBRASKA

MINNESOTA

WISCONSIN
St. Paul
Madison

IOWA
Des Moines
Lincoln

KANSAS
Topeka

Lake Superior

MICHIGAN
Lake Michigan
Lansing

Lake Huron

ILLINOIS
Chicago
Springfield

INDIANA
Indianapolis

OHIO
Columbus

Jefferson City

Missouri

MISSOURI

OKLAHOMA
Oklahoma City

Mississippi

KENTUCKY
Frankfort

TENNESSEE
Nashville

Little Rock
ARKANSAS

Ohio

WEST VIRGINIA
Charleston

Lake Ontario
Lake Erie

NEW YORK
Albany

MAINE
Augusta

Montpelier
VERMONT
NEW HAMPSHIRE
Concord
MASS. Boston
Hartford
CONN. R.I. Providence

PENNSYLVANIA
Harrisburg
N.J. New York City
Trenton
Philadelphia
Annapolis Dover
Washington, D.C.
MD. DEL.

APPALACHIAN MOUNTAINS

VIRGINIA
Richmond

Raleigh

NORTH CAROLINA

ATLANTIC OCEAN

TEXAS
Austin
Houston

Rio Grande

MEXICO

Mississippi

Baton Rouge
LOUISIANA

Jackson
MISSISSIPPI

ALABAMA
Montgomery

GEORGIA
Atlanta

Columbia
SOUTH CAROLINA

Tallahassee

FLORIDA

Gulf of Mexico

The Capitol and the White House are buildings in Washington, D.C. The White House is the president's home. The president also works there. The people who make laws work in the Capitol, shown here. It is easy to spot the Capitol because it has a dome.

THE BAHAMAS

CUBA

HAITI DOMINICAN REPUBLIC PUERTO RICO (USA)

CARIBBEAN SEA

0   125   250   375 miles

Population: 290,350,000
Language: English (some Spanish)
Capital: Washington, D.C.
Average person's buying power: $37,600
Land area: 3,717,810 square miles
Major cities: New York, Los Angeles, Chicago, Houston, Philadelphia, Phoenix, San Diego
Unit of currency: U.S. dollar
Industries: diverse manufacturing, steel, motor vehicles, aerospace, telecommunications
Agricultural products: beef cattle, dairy products, wheat, pork, corn

United States (West)

The western United States stretches from the Rocky Mountains in the east to the Pacific Ocean in the west. It reaches to Canada in the north and to Mexico in the south. This area has some of North America's most spectacular scenery. The world's largest gorge, the Grand Canyon, lies in Arizona.

California lies along the coast of the Pacific Ocean. It is home to more people than any other state. Hawaii, which lies in the middle of the Pacific Ocean, is made up of 137 islands. They were formed by undersea volcanoes. To the far northwest lies Alaska. Alaska has more land than any other state. Canada separates Alaska from the rest of the United States.

The Golden Gate Bridge is in San Francisco. Do you recognize it? It is one of California's most familiar landmarks. It spans the channel between San Francisco Bay and the Pacific Ocean. The bridge is 8,981 feet long.

The Grand Canyon

The Grand Canyon is one of the natural wonders of the world. It is located in Arizona. The world's largest gorge, it is 277 miles long. At places it can be up to 18 miles wide. It is more than one mile deep.

The Grand Canyon is a great example of water erosion, which happens when water slowly wears away at something, such as rock. Over millions of years, the Colorado River has worn away at the rock around it to form the Grand Canyon.

Nearly four million people visit the Grand Canyon each year. They come to enjoy the incredible views!

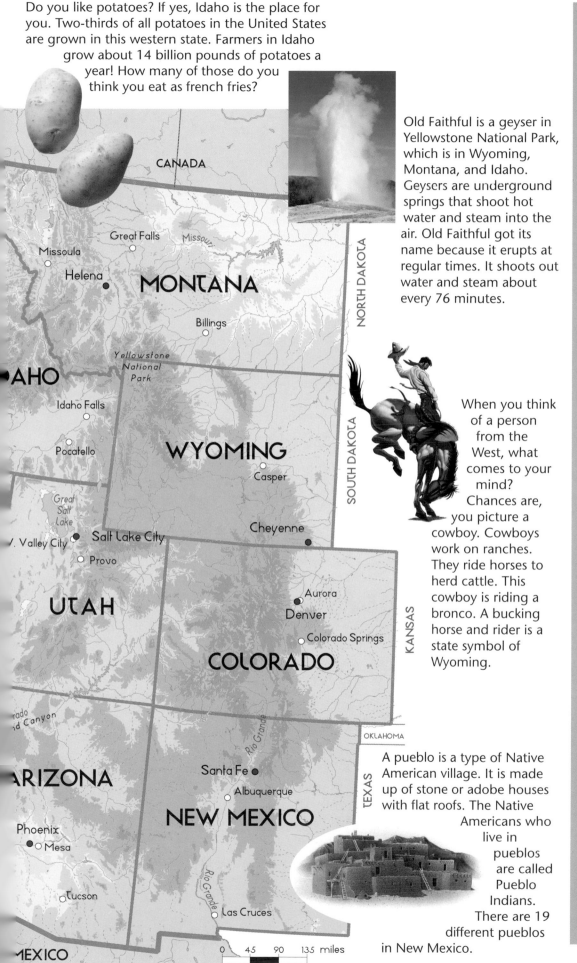

Do you like potatoes? If yes, Idaho is the place for you. Two-thirds of all potatoes in the United States are grown in this western state. Farmers in Idaho grow about 14 billion pounds of potatoes a year! How many of those do you think you eat as french fries?

Old Faithful is a geyser in Yellowstone National Park, which is in Wyoming, Montana, and Idaho. Geysers are underground springs that shoot hot water and steam into the air. Old Faithful got its name because it erupts at regular times. It shoots out water and steam about every 76 minutes.

When you think of a person from the West, what comes to your mind? Chances are, you picture a cowboy. Cowboys work on ranches. They ride horses to herd cattle. This cowboy is riding a bronco. A bucking horse and rider is a state symbol of Wyoming.

A pueblo is a type of Native American village. It is made up of stone or adobe houses with flat roofs. The Native Americans who live in pueblos are called Pueblo Indians. There are 19 different pueblos in New Mexico.

Alaska
Population: 640,000
Capital: Juneau
Major cities: Anchorage, Fairbanks

Arizona
Population: 5,310,000
Capital: Phoenix
Major cities: Phoenix, Tucson, Mesa

California
Population: 34,510,000
Capital: Sacramento
Major cities: Los Angeles, San Diego, San Jose, San Francisco

Colorado
Population: 4,420,000
Capital: Denver
Major cities: Denver, Colorado Springs, Aurora

Hawaii
Population: 1,230,000
Capital: Honolulu
Major cities: Honolulu, Hilo

Idaho
Population: 1,330,000
Capital: Boise
Major cities: Boise, Pocatello, Idaho Falls

Montana
Population: 910,000
Capital: Helena
Major cities: Billings, Great Falls, Missoula

Nevada
Population: 2,110,000
Capital: Carson City
Major cities: Las Vegas, Reno, Henderson

New Mexico
Population: 1,830,000
Capital: Santa Fe
Major cities: Albuquerque, Las Cruces, Santa Fe

Oregon
Population: 3,480,000
Capital: Salem
Major cities: Portland, Eugene, Salem

Utah
Population: 2,270,000
Capital: Salt Lake City
Major cities: Salt Lake City, West Valley City, Provo

Washington
Population: 5,990,000
Capital: Olympia
Major cities: Seattle, Spokane, Tacoma

Wyoming
Population: 500,000
Capital: Cheyenne
Major cities: Cheyenne, Casper

United States (Midwest)

The Midwest has 12 states. Prairie, a kind of flat land, covers most of this area. This part of the country is rich in natural resources. These include coal and soil that is good for farming. Farmland covers a lot of the Midwest. In some places, such as Iowa and Nebraska, you can see wheat and cornfields stretching for miles and miles. Most of the Great Lakes sit in the northeastern area of the Midwest.

Near Mount Rushmore there is another statue in a cliff. It is of Crazy Horse, an Oglala Sioux Indian chief. He led his people in a fight against settlers moving into their land. Korczak Ziolkowski started the sculpture of Crazy Horse in 1948. He died in 1982, but his family continues his work today.

Ilinois
Population: 12,490,000
Capital: Springfield
Major cities: Chicago, Rockford, Aurora, Peoria

Indiana
Population: 6,120,000
Capital: Indianapolis
Major cities: Indianapolis, Fort Wayne, Gary

Iowa
Population: 2,930,000
Capital: Des Moines
Major cities: Des Moines, Cedar Rapids, Davenport

Kansas
Population: 2,700,000
Capital: Topeka
Major cities: Wichita, Overland Park, Kansas City

Michigan
Population: 10,000,000
Capital: Lansing
Major cities: Detroit, Grand Rapids, Warren

Minnesota
Population: 4,980,000
Capital: St. Paul
Major cities: Minneapolis, St. Paul, Duluth

Missouri
Population: 5,630,000
Capital: Jefferson City
Major cities: Kansas City, St. Louis, Springfield

Nebraska
Population: 1,720,000
Capital: Lincoln
Major cities: Omaha, Lincoln

North Dakota
Population: 640,000
Capital: Bismarck
Major cities: Fargo, Bismarck

Ohio
Population: 11,380,000
Capital: Columbus
Major cities: Columbus, Cleveland, Cincinnati, Toledo

South Dakota
Population: 760,000
Capital: Pierre
Major cities: Sioux Falls, Rapid City

Wisconsin
Population: 5,410,000
Capital: Madison
Major cities: Milwaukee, Madison, Green Bay

The United States produces a lot of wheat. Most of this wheat grows in the Midwest. Just west of Iowa is a "wheat belt." Here, huge fields of wheat cover the land as far as the eye can see.

CANADA

MONTANA

Minot

NORTH DAKOT

Bismarck

Missouri

Pierre

Rapid City

SOUTH DAKO

WYOMING

Mount Rushmore

NEBRASKA

COLORADO

KANSAS

Wisconsin is known as America's Dairyland. Do you know why? Because it is one of the leading milk-producing states. Thousands of milk cows graze on the rich, green grass that covers the land. Wisconsin dairy also includes cheese and butter.

Mount Rushmore

Some of the largest carved figures in the world are in the Black Hills of South Dakota. Here, the faces of four U.S. presidents—George Washington, Thomas Jefferson, Theodore Roosevelt, and Abraham Lincoln—have been chiseled into a rocky cliff called Mount Rushmore. The head of Washington is as tall as a five-story building!

In 1927, American sculptor Gutzon Borglum began work on Mount Rushmore. He and his workers used drills and dynamite to cut faces into the cliff. They worked for 14 years. Borglum died in 1941 before Mount Rushmore was complete. His son, Lincoln, finished the work we see today.

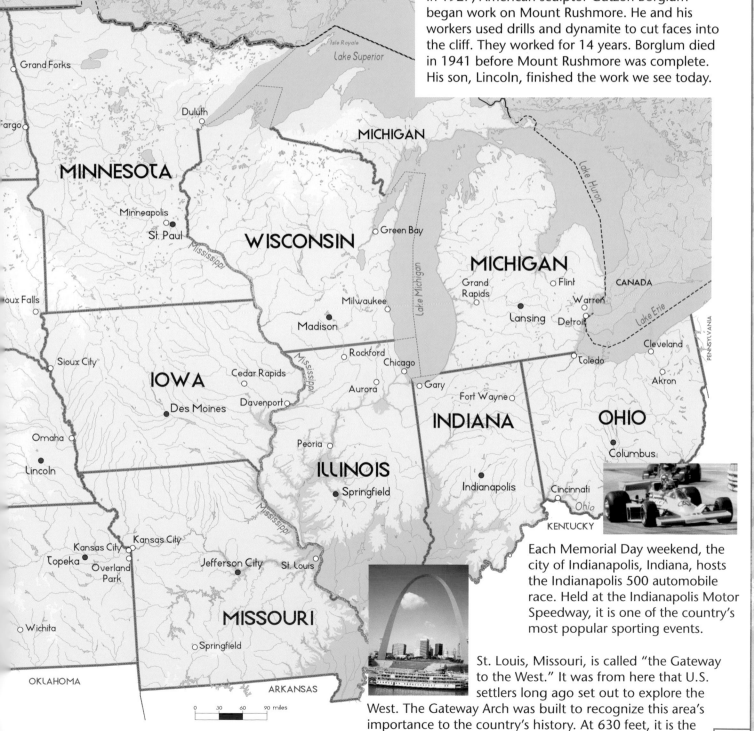

Each Memorial Day weekend, the city of Indianapolis, Indiana, hosts the Indianapolis 500 automobile race. Held at the Indianapolis Motor Speedway, it is one of the country's most popular sporting events.

St. Louis, Missouri, is called "the Gateway to the West." It was from here that U.S. settlers long ago set out to explore the West. The Gateway Arch was built to recognize this area's importance to the country's history. At 630 feet, it is the tallest human-made monument in the United States.

19

United States (South)

Some of the warmest weather in the United States is in the South. Much of the land here is covered with plains, rivers, swamps, and lagoons. Sixteen states make up the South. The nation's capital, Washington, D.C., is here, too. Texas is the second biggest U.S. state, after Alaska. Beef and oil industries are located here. Many rivers cross the southern United States, including the mighty Mississippi, one of North America's longest rivers. The beaches along the Atlantic Ocean and the Gulf of Mexico are fun to visit.

Alabama
Population: 4,470,000
Capital: Montgomery
Major cities: Birmingham, Montgomery, Mobile

Arkansas
Population: 2,700,000
Capital: Little Rock
Major cities: Little Rock, Fort Smith

Delaware
Population: 800,000
Capital: Dover
Major city: Wilmington

Florida
Population: 16,400,000
Capital: Tallahassee
Major cities: Jacksonville, Miami, Tampa, St. Petersburg, Orlando

Georgia
Population: 8,390,000
Capital: Atlanta
Major cities: Atlanta, Augusta, Columbus

Kentucky
Population: 4,070,000
Capital: Frankfort
Major cities: Louisville, Lexington

Louisiana
Population: 4,470,000
Capital: Baton Rouge
Major cities: New Orleans, Baton Rouge, Shreveport

Maryland
Population: 5,380,000
Capital: Annapolis
Major cities: Baltimore, Frederick

Mississippi
Population: 2,860,000
Capital: Jackson
Major cities: Jackson, Gulfport

North Carolina
Population: 8,190,000
Capital: Raleigh
Major cities: Charlotte, Raleigh, Greensboro

Oklahoma
Population: 3,470,000
Capital: Oklahoma City
Major cities: Oklahoma City, Tulsa, Norman

South Carolina
Population: 4,070,000
Capital: Columbia
Major cities: Columbia, Charleston, Greenville

Tennessee
Population: 5,750,000
Capital: Nashville
Major cities: Memphis, Nashville, Knoxville, Chattanooga

Texas
Population: 21,330,000
Capital: Austin
Major cities: Houston, Dallas, San Antonio, Austin

Virginia
Population: 7,190,000
Capital: Richmond
Major cities: Virginia Beach, Norfolk, Chesapeake, Richmond

West Virginia
Population: 1,810,000
Capital: Charleston
Major cities: Charleston, Huntington

COLORADO

KANSAS

NEW MEXICO

Tul:

OKLAHOM

Oklahoma City

Norman

Dall

El Paso

TEXAS

Austin

San Antonio

MEXICO

Brownsville

You may see them all across Texas and Oklahoma. They move up and down, up and down. What are they? They are oil rigs. Like huge pumps, they pump oil out from deep inside the earth. This oil is used to make gasoline and other products.

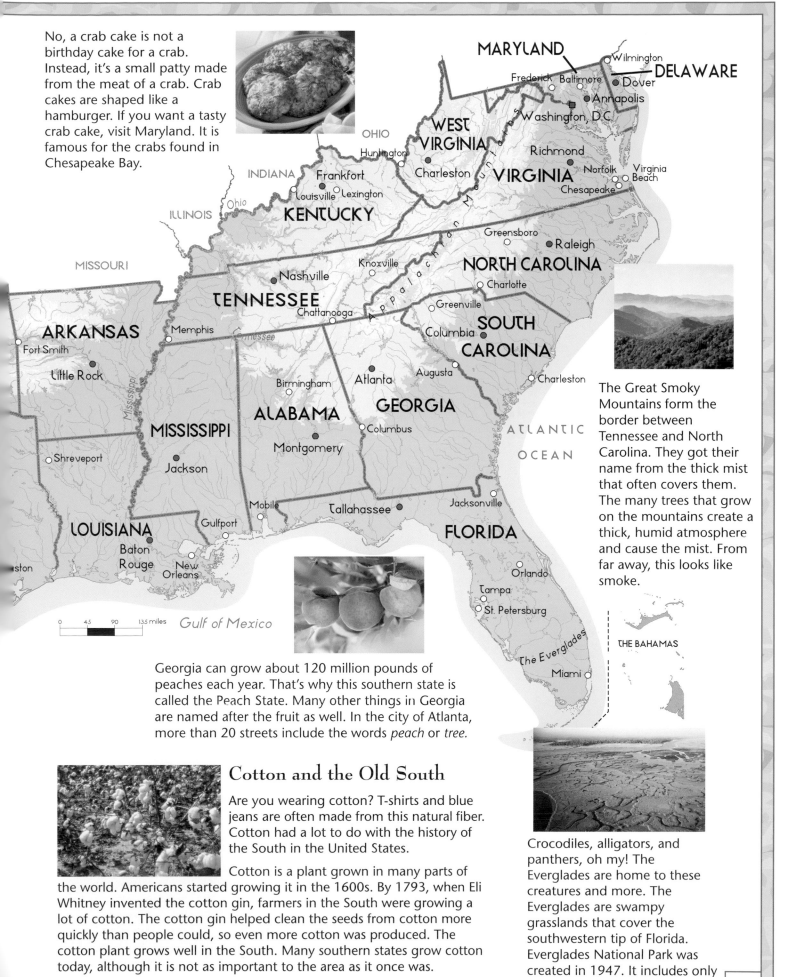

No, a crab cake is not a birthday cake for a crab. Instead, it's a small patty made from the meat of a crab. Crab cakes are shaped like a hamburger. If you want a tasty crab cake, visit Maryland. It is famous for the crabs found in Chesapeake Bay.

The Great Smoky Mountains form the border between Tennessee and North Carolina. They got their name from the thick mist that often covers them. The many trees that grow on the mountains create a thick, humid atmosphere and cause the mist. From far away, this looks like smoke.

Georgia can grow about 120 million pounds of peaches each year. That's why this southern state is called the Peach State. Many other things in Georgia are named after the fruit as well. In the city of Atlanta, more than 20 streets include the words *peach* or *tree*.

Cotton and the Old South

Are you wearing cotton? T-shirts and blue jeans are often made from this natural fiber. Cotton had a lot to do with the history of the South in the United States.

Cotton is a plant grown in many parts of the world. Americans started growing it in the 1600s. By 1793, when Eli Whitney invented the cotton gin, farmers in the South were growing a lot of cotton. The cotton gin helped clean the seeds from cotton more quickly than people could, so even more cotton was produced. The cotton plant grows well in the South. Many southern states grow cotton today, although it is not as important to the area as it once was.

Crocodiles, alligators, and panthers, oh my! The Everglades are home to these creatures and more. The Everglades are swampy grasslands that cover the southwestern tip of Florida. Everglades National Park was created in 1947. It includes only a small part of the Everglades.

21

United States (Northeast)

The biggest city in the United States, New York City, is in the northeast. It is one of the world's main places of business and culture. It was even the nation's capital before Washington, D.C.! Other great cities also lie along or near the Atlantic Ocean in the Northeast, such as Boston, Massachusetts, and Philadelphia, Pennsylvania. The Appalachian Mountains separate the Northeast from the Midwest. They stretch for about 1,500 miles, from Alabama to Maine and into Canada. New England lies in the far northeast corner of the United States. The area got its name because its beautiful scenery reminded early settlers of their homeland, England.

Niagara Falls is a waterfall on New York's Niagara River. It is one of the most beautiful natural wonders of North America. Niagara Falls is on the border between the United States and Canada. Each country is home to a part of the falls.

Empire State Building

One building in the New York City skyline that is easy to recognize is the Empire State Building. The top of the building is a tower.

A metal lightning rod caps it off. From the ground to the tip of the lightning rod, it is more than 1,450 feet tall. Under the tower are 102 floors. The Empire State Building was built in 1931. For more than 40 years, it was the tallest building in the world.

Pittsburgh, Pennsylvania, was once home to so many steelmakers that it earned the nickname Steeltown. Steel is used to make many things, such as cars and buildings. Today, the Pittsburgh area does not make as much steel. The football team in Pittsburgh is called the Steelers.

Lake Ontario

Rochester

Niagara Falls

Buffalo

Lake Erie

PENNSYLVANIA

OHIO

Pittsburgh

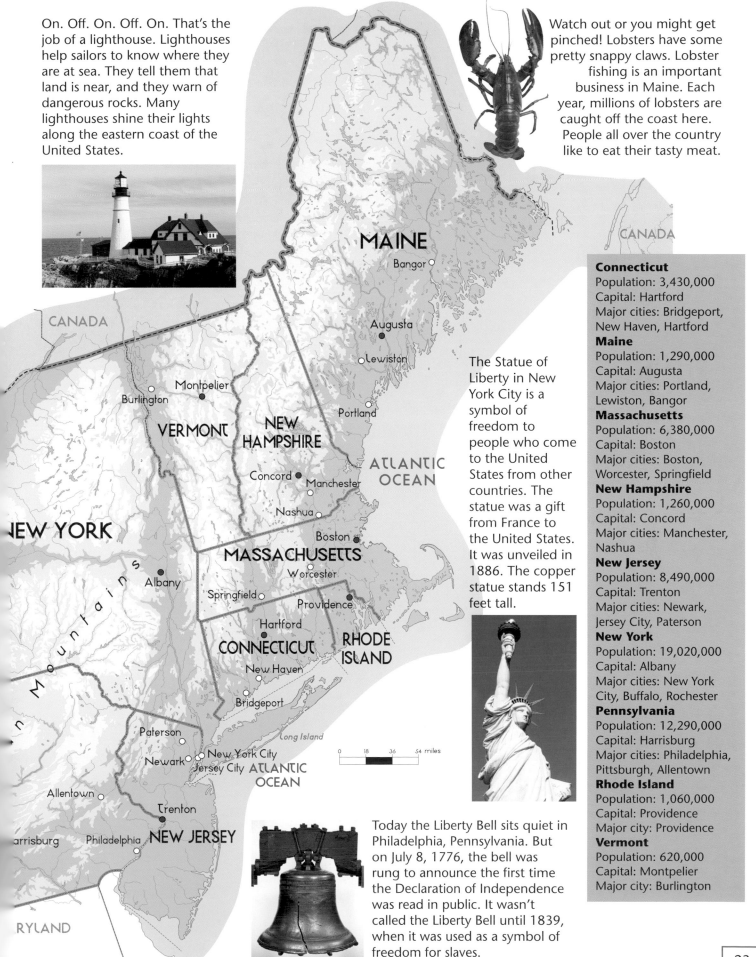

On. Off. On. Off. On. That's the job of a lighthouse. Lighthouses help sailors to know where they are at sea. They tell them that land is near, and they warn of dangerous rocks. Many lighthouses shine their lights along the eastern coast of the United States.

Watch out or you might get pinched! Lobsters have some pretty snappy claws. Lobster fishing is an important business in Maine. Each year, millions of lobsters are caught off the coast here. People all over the country like to eat their tasty meat.

The Statue of Liberty in New York City is a symbol of freedom to people who come to the United States from other countries. The statue was a gift from France to the United States. It was unveiled in 1886. The copper statue stands 151 feet tall.

Connecticut
Population: 3,430,000
Capital: Hartford
Major cities: Bridgeport, New Haven, Hartford
Maine
Population: 1,290,000
Capital: Augusta
Major cities: Portland, Lewiston, Bangor
Massachusetts
Population: 6,380,000
Capital: Boston
Major cities: Boston, Worcester, Springfield
New Hampshire
Population: 1,260,000
Capital: Concord
Major cities: Manchester, Nashua
New Jersey
Population: 8,490,000
Capital: Trenton
Major cities: Newark, Jersey City, Paterson
New York
Population: 19,020,000
Capital: Albany
Major cities: New York City, Buffalo, Rochester
Pennsylvania
Population: 12,290,000
Capital: Harrisburg
Major cities: Philadelphia, Pittsburgh, Allentown
Rhode Island
Population: 1,060,000
Capital: Providence
Major city: Providence
Vermont
Population: 620,000
Capital: Montpelier
Major city: Burlington

Today the Liberty Bell sits quiet in Philadelphia, Pennsylvania. But on July 8, 1776, the bell was rung to announce the first time the Declaration of Independence was read in public. It wasn't called the Liberty Bell until 1839, when it was used as a symbol of freedom for slaves.

Canada

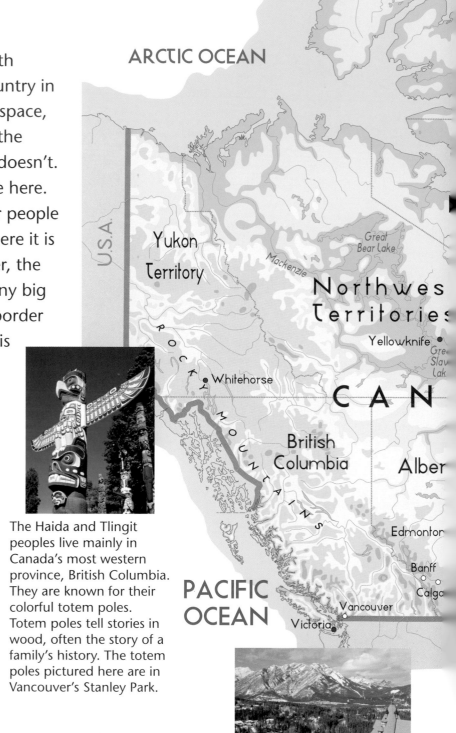

Canada covers almost half of North America. It is the second-biggest country in the world, after Russia. With all that space, you might think Canada has one of the biggest populations in the world. It doesn't. Just more than 30 million people live here. Much of this vast land is too cold for people to live on it. Most Canadians live where it is warmer, along the St. Lawrence River, the Great Lakes, and the west coast. Many big cities are located close to Canada's border with the United States. The country is divided into provinces, which are similar to U.S. states.

Québec

If you hear people speaking French, does that mean you are in France? Not necessarily! Most of the people in the province of Québec speak French. Québec is the largest province in Canada. The

people here come mostly from French families. That's because French settlers came to the Québec area during the 1600s and 1700s.

The capital of Québec is Québec City. One part of town called Old Québec looks like a European city. French Canadians are very proud of their heritage.

The Haida and Tlingit peoples live mainly in Canada's most western province, British Columbia. They are known for their colorful totem poles. Totem poles tell stories in wood, often the story of a family's history. The totem poles pictured here are in Vancouver's Stanley Park.

The Rocky Mountains are the largest mountain system in North America. They stretch for more than 3,000 miles. They rise in both the United States and Canada. Banff National Park sits in the Rocky Mountains in Alberta. This is the oldest national park in Canada.

The Inuit have lived in Canada for thousands of years. This was their home when Europeans arrived. Today they live in the far northern territory of Nunavut. Most native peoples of Canada now live in modern communities.

Population: 32,210,000
Languages: English, French
Capital: Ottawa
Average person's buying power: $29,400
Land area: 3,851,810 square miles
Unit of currency: Canadian dollar
Major cities: Toronto, Montréal, Vancouver
Industrial products: transportation equipment, chemicals, wood and paper products, fish products, petroleum and natural gas
Agricultural products: wheat, barley, dairy products, forest products, fish

Ice hockey is one of Canada's most popular sports. It developed in the 1800s. Many people have claimed to invent it, but no one knows for sure. If you want to be a hockey player, start now. Many young Canadians start competing at just four or five years old!

navut Territory

Iqaluit

Mackenzie

Hudson Bay

Manitoba

skatchewan

Ontario

Québec

Newfoundland

Lake Winnipeg

Regina

Winnipeg

NITED STATES

Lake Superior

St. Lawrence

Québec City

Prince Edward Island

St. John's

New Brunswick

Montréal

Fredericton

Charlottetown

Lake Michigan

Lake Huron

Ottawa

Toronto

Lake Ontario

Halifax

Nova Scotia

Lake Erie

ATLANTIC OCEAN

Canada has about 250,000 farms. More than half are in the prairie provinces in the center of the country. These provinces include Manitoba, Saskatchewan, and Alberta. The main crop here is wheat.

0   180   360   540 miles

Mexico

Mexico is a long and narrow country. It is slightly less than three times the size of Texas. This North American country sits just south of the United States. The countries share a 2,000-mile border. The Pacific Ocean is on Mexico's western border. The Gulf of Mexico is on the east.

Mexico is a land of very different landscapes and climates. You do not have to travel far to see big changes in the weather and land.

Plants can grow on only some of Mexico's land. This is because the weather is so dry and there are many mountains. However, Mexicans still grow many crops, especially on the coasts and central highlands.

Population: 104,910,000
Language: Spanish
Capital: Mexico City
Average person's buying power: $9,000
Land area: 761,610 square miles
Unit of currency: Mexican peso
Major cities: Mexico City, Guadalajara, Monterrey
Industrial products: food and beverages, tobacco, chemicals, iron and steel, petroleum
Agricultural products: corn, wheat, soybeans, beef, wood products

UNITED STATES

Tijuana
Nogales
Ciudad Juárez
Guadalupe Mexico
Baja California
Gulf of California
Yaqui
Chihuahua
Conchos
MEXICO
Sierra Madre Occidental
La Paz
Mazatlán
Río Grande de S.
PACIFIC OCEAN
Guadalajara

The eagle sitting on a cactus eating a snake is the symbol of the country. That is why it is on Mexico's flag. According to legend, the Aztecs searched for such an eagle. When they found it, they built their capital right on that spot. Over the centuries, this Aztec settlement grew into Mexico City.

People from around the world flock to Mexico for vacations. They come to enjoy the warm weather and sandy beaches. Many beach resorts, such as Acapulco and Cancún, are along both coasts of Mexico.

Areas of northern Mexico are covered with desert. But even in this dry climate, many plants thrive here. They include more than 1,000 different kinds of cacti. These sturdy plants survive by storing water in their stems. The giant cactus, or saguaro, grows so tall it looks like a tree.

Many different ancient peoples lived on the land that is now Mexico. More than 3,000 years ago, the Olmec ruled the land. Others followed them. They include the Teotihuacán, the Mayan, and the Aztec. These cultures built huge buildings and cities that were later abandoned or conquered by Spanish explorers.

Mexico City

Mexico City is the capital of Mexico. Hundreds of years ago, it was called Tenochtitlán and was the capital of the Aztec people. Now it has one of the largest populations in the world, with more than 18 million people living in or near the city. That's about one-fifth of Mexico's total population. With all those people, there is a lot to see in Mexico City. Chapultepec Park is home to a forest, a castle, an amusement park, and many museums.

Rio Grande

Matamoroso
○Monterrey

Gulf of Mexico

○Xalapa
Mexico City
○Veracruz

Puebla de Zaragoza
Balsas
Sierra Madre Del Sur
capulco○
Oaxaca

Chiapas

M a y a s

Yucatán

○Cancún

Chetumal

BELIZE

GUATEMALA

CUBA

CARIBBEAN SEA

0   90   180   270 miles

Tropical forests cover the southern areas of Mexico. The tops of the tall trees here form a thick canopy, or cover. This keeps most light from reaching the forest floor. A rich variety of animals live in the Mexican forest. Here you will find ocelots, spider monkeys, and iguanas.

These Mexican children are wearing traditional folk-dancing costumes. The boy's black suit is called a charro. His hat is a sombrero. It has a very wide brim. Girls' dresses usually have a lot of lace and ribbon. You can see folk dancing during festivals and celebrations.

Caribbean

The Caribbean Sea is an area just east of Central America that has hundreds of islands. Many of these islands are independent countries.

The Caribbean Sea is part of the Atlantic Ocean. Tropical forests used to cover most of these islands. The people here have cleared away most of these trees to build farms. They make money by growing fruits and vegetables.

Many people from all over the world like to visit the Caribbean. They enjoy the sandy beaches, the beautiful scenery, and the warm weather.

Christopher Columbus landed on an island in 1493. He named it San Juan, but it was later renamed Puerto Rico. Today, the United States controls Puerto Rico and part of the nearby Virgin Islands. While they are not states, they hold many of the same rights as a state.

UNITED STATES

Gulf of Mexico

Nassa

Havana

MEXICO

CUBA

JAMAICA

King

CENTRAL AMERICA

Coral Reefs

Would you like to visit a rain forest under the sea? That's how people describe the coral reefs that lie in the Caribbean Sea. Coral reefs and rain forests are both colorful worlds with thousands of plants and animals.

People dive down to visit the coral reefs. Swimming through a reef is like finding your way through a maze.

Coral reefs grow only in warm, salty waters. Millions of tiny creatures build them. Sadly, coral reefs are in danger! Climate changes and pollution are making them sick. People are working to help save them.

The Caribbean is a great place to make fruit salad. Many tropical fruits grow here, such as bananas, coconuts, mangoes, papayas, and pineapples. Long ago, European settlers brought these fruit trees to the islands to grow. Today the islands wouldn't be the same without them.

If you like candy, you'd probably like growing sugarcane. Sugarcane has long been Cuba's most important crop. This island country is one of the world's leading producers of sugar. Sugarcane has stalks that contain a juice from which sugar is made.

Antigua and Barbuda
Population: 70,000
Language: English
Capital: St. John's
Average person's buying power: $11,000

The Bahamas
Population: 300,000
Language: English (some Creole)
Capital: Nassau
Average person's buying power: $17,000

Barbados
Population: 280,000
Language: English
Capital: Bridgetown
Average person's buying power: $14,500

Cuba
Population: 11,270,000
Language: Spanish
Capital: Havana
Average person's buying power: $2,300

Dominica
Population: 70,000
Language: English (some French Creole)
Capital: Roseau
Average person's buying power: $5,400

Dominican Republic
Population: 8,720,000
Language: Spanish
Capital: Santo Domingo
Average person's buying power: $6,100

Grenada
Population: 90,000
Language: English (some French Creole)
Capital: Saint George's
Average person's buying power: $5,000

Haiti
Population: 7,530,000
Languages: Haitian Creole, French
Capital: Port-au-Prince
Average person's buying power: $1,700

Jamaica
Population: 2,700,000
Language: English
Capital: Kingston
Average person's buying power: $3,900

Saint Kitts and Nevis
Population: 40,000
Language: English
Capital: Basseterre
Average person's buying power: $8,800

Saint Lucia
Population: 170,000
Language: English (some French Creole)
Capital: Castries
Average person's buying power: $5,400

Saint Vincent and the Grenadines
Population: 120,000
Language: English (some French Creole)
Capital: Kingstown
Average person's buying power: $2,900

Trinidad and Tobago
Population: 1,110,000
Language: English (some Hindi, French, Spanish, Chinese)
Capital: Port-of-Spain
Average person's buying power: $9,500

ATLANTIC OCEAN

THE BAHAMAS

DOMINICAN REPUBLIC

HAITI

Port-au-Prince

Santo Domingo

San Juan

PUERTO RICO (U.S.A.)

SAINT KITTS AND NEVIS

ANTIGUA AND BARBUDA

DOMINICA

CARIBBEAN SEA

SAINT VINCENT AND THE GRENADINES

SAINT LUCIA

BARBADOS

GRENADA

Port-of-Spain

TRINIDAD AND TOBAGO

SOUTH AMERICA

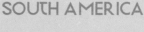

0   180   360   540 miles

Drums are important to the music of the Caribbean Islands. Calypso music from Trinidad is usually played by a steel band. A steel band is a group of drums originally made from empty steel oil containers. They are also called pans. The musician uses sticks to play them.

The peoples of the Caribbean invented many styles of music, such as reggae, calypso, and salsa. These different styles combine native, African, and Spanish music. Calypso includes traditional songs of Trinidad. Salsa is dance music from Cuba. Reggae started in Jamaica.

Looking at a beach in the Caribbean is like looking at a postcard. The scenery is so beautiful. Not all the beaches look alike, however. Some have white coral sand. Others have fine, black volcanic sand.

Central America

Central America is a thin strip of land connecting North and South America. Central America is divided into seven countries.

Many people in Central America live on small farms, where they grow their own food. There is not a lot of room for farms, however. Most of the land is covered with mountains. Many are active volcanoes. Earthquakes and volcanoes sometimes strike the region. Rain forests used to cover much of southern Central America.

Long ago, the Mayan people lived in what is now southern Mexico, Belize, and Guatemala. Even today, you can tell they were here. Some of their descendants live in the mountains. And ruins of their ancient buildings still stand. Many tourists come to study and enjoy these ruins each year.

Most of the farmers of Central America live in tiny villages. They grow vegetables, bananas, and other crops. Some farmers sell their crops at markets, such as the one shown in this picture. Other farmers farm only enough food for their own families.

Belize
Population: 270,000
Language: English (some Spanish, Mayan, Garifuna, Creole)
Capital: Belmopan
Average person's buying power: $4,900

Costa Rica
Population: 3,900,000
Language: Spanish
Capital: San José
Average person's buying power: $8,500

El Salvador
Population: 6,480,000
Language: Spanish
Capital: San Salvador
Average person's buying power: $4,700

Guatemala
Population: 13,910,000
Language: Spanish (some Mayan languages)
Capital: Guatemala City
Average person's buying power: $3,700

Honduras
Population: 6,670,000
Language: Spanish (some Mayan languages)
Capital: Tegucigalpa
Average person's buying power: $2,600

Nicaragua
Population: 5,130,000
Language: Spanish
Capital: Managua
Average person's buying power: $2,500

Panama
Population: 2,970,000
Language: Spanish (some English)
Capital: Panama City
Average person's buying power: $6,000

Would you like to explore the deep sea? How about hop on a jet ski? Or would you rather swing on a hammock stretched between two palm trees? You can do all this and more at beach resorts in Belize. There is something for all fans of the water and beach.

Do you like to eat bananas? Well, you won't go hungry in Honduras! This yellow fruit is very important to the people here. Many grow bananas to be sold to other countries.

Panama Canal

The Panama Canal is a waterway that links the Atlantic and Pacific Oceans. It opened in 1914. Before the canal was built, ships had to sail all the way around South America. That's a trip of 8,700 miles! The canal itself is only about 51 miles long. Thousands of ships use it.

When the canal was built, disease was a big problem. Many workers died of malaria. Mosquitoes spread the disease. The early years of canal building were spent ridding the land of bushes, swamps, and large areas of grass. This is where mosquitoes like to live. When these disappeared, malaria deaths were greatly reduced.

ONDURAS

Tegucigalpa ■

NICARAGUA

Managua ■

Lake Nicaragua

CARIBBEAN SEA

ACIFIC
CEAN

COSTA RICA

San José ■

Plants and animals of rain forests are in danger. Many are losing their homes to humans. Costa Rica is trying to fix this. More than one-fourth of Costa Rica's land has been set aside for national parks, reserves, and protected areas. Here, the plants and animals are protected.

Panama Canal

Panama City ■

PANAMA

SOUTH AMERICA

0   20   40   60 miles

Spain ruled much of Central America for years. That's why many of the buildings have a Spanish look to them. The cities are set up like Spanish cities, too. They center around a Catholic church. Religion is very important in the everyday lives of the people here.

South America

NORTH AMERICA

CARIBBEAN SEA

VENEZUELA

SURINAME

FRENCH GUIANA (FRANCE)

GUYANA

COLOMBIA

BRAZIL

ECUADOR

PERU

BOLIVIA

PACIFIC OCEAN

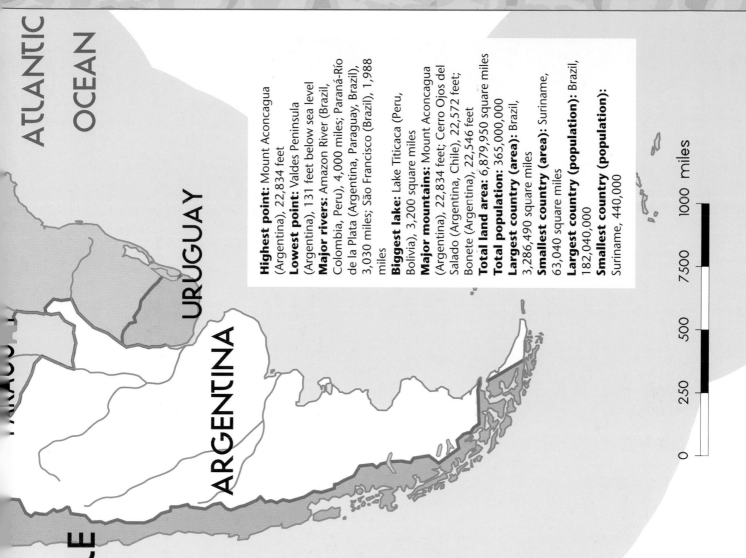

ATLANTIC OCEAN

URUGUAY

ARGENTINA

CHILE

Highest point: Mount Aconcagua (Argentina), 22,834 feet
Lowest point: Valdes Peninsula (Argentina), 131 feet below sea level
Major rivers: Amazon River (Brazil, Colombia, Peru), 4,000 miles; Paraná-Río de la Plata (Argentina, Paraguay, Brazil), 3,030 miles; São Francisco (Brazil), 1,988 miles
Biggest lake: Lake Titicaca (Peru, Bolivia), 3,200 square miles
Major mountains: Mount Aconcagua (Argentina), 22,834 feet; Cerro Ojos del Salado (Argentina, Chile), 22,572 feet; Bonete (Argentina), 22,546 feet
Total land area: 6,879,950 square miles
Total population: 365,000,000
Largest country (area): Brazil, 3,286,490 square miles
Smallest country (area): Suriname, 63,040 square miles
Largest country (population): Brazil, 182,040,000
Smallest country (population): Suriname, 440,000

0   250   500   750   1000 miles

South America is the fourth-largest continent in area. It covers about one-eighth of the world's land area and is divided into 13 different countries and dependencies.

If you like variety, South America may be for you. You can find almost every type of weather and landscape here. The world's largest tropical rain forest is on this continent, as is one of the driest places in the world. The equator runs through South America, but the southern tip of the continent is only 600 miles from Antarctica.

Do you like snow...or volcanoes? You can find both along the Andes Mountains. These majestic mountains run down the entire western edge of South America to form the longest mountain chain in the world.

South America is almost completely surrounded by water. The Caribbean Sea lies to the north. The Atlantic Ocean borders the coast to the east. The Pacific Ocean lies along the west coast of the continent.

Long ago, Spain and Portugal ruled most of South America. That's why today so many people here speak Spanish or Portuguese.

33

Northern South America

Four countries and one dependency round the northern corner of South America. The largest is Colombia, a country known for its coffee. It borders the Pacific Ocean and the Caribbean Sea in the Atlantic. East of it is Venezuela. Since oil was found here, this country has become more wealthy. To its east is Guyana. The many mountains here make most of the land hard to reach. Next is Suriname, the smallest country in South America. Beside it is French Guiana. French Guiana is not actually a country. It is a dependency governed by France.

Bogotá is a city of opposites. It is the capital of Colombia. Modern towers rise from the flat land. The city sits next to hills and mountains. In some areas, people are rich and live in nice houses. In other areas, people are poor and live in shacks.

Caracas

Maracaibo

PANAMA

Magdalena

Medellín

Meta

Bogotá

Orinoco

Cali

COLOMBIA

Andes

ECUADOR

PERU

What could this statue be? That's what people in San Agustin, Colombia, have been asking for years. Hundreds of these huge sculptures of people and animals dot the land here. People who lived in this area thousands of years ago built them. But why? No one knows for sure.

Simón Bolívar

Some people called Simón Bolívar the George Washington of South America. That tells you he did something for his country. In fact, he did something for many countries in South America.

Simón Bolívar was one of South America's greatest generals. In the early 1800s, he helped Bolivia, Colombia, Ecuador, Peru, and Venezuela become free. Until then, Spain had ruled all of these countries.

Bolívar was born in Caracas, Venezuela, in 1783. He died in 1830. In 1825, Upper Peru became a country called Bolivia. It was given this name in honor of Bolívar.

GRENADA

TRINIDAD AND TOBAGO

0   30   60   90 miles

ATLANTIC OCEAN

Orinoco

VENEZUELA

Georgetown

Paramaribo

GUYANA

Cayenne

SURINAME

FRENCH GUIANA (FRANCE)

BRAZIL

Some of the adults you know probably drink coffee. Their cup of coffee may have come from Colombia. The beans grow on coffee trees like these shown in the picture. More than 500,000 farms in Colombia grow coffee trees.

Small villages are scattered across northern South America. The homes here usually have only one or two rooms. Many villagers are farmers. They flock to outdoor markets across the countryside to sell their crops. Farmers often ship their crops to these markets in boats on rivers.

Colombia
Population: 41,670,000
Language: Spanish
Capital: Bogotá
Average person's buying power: $6,500
Guyana
Population: 710,000
Language: English
Capital: Georgetown
Average person's buying power: $4,000
Suriname
Population: 440,000
Language: Dutch (some English, Sranang Tongo)
Capital: Paramaribo
Average person's buying power: $3,500
Venezuela
Population: 24,660,000
Language: Spanish
Capital: Caracas
Average person's buying power: $5,500

Andean South America

Andean South America is made up of three countries, Peru, Ecuador, and Bolivia. Peru and Ecuador lie along the Pacific Ocean. The Andes Mountains run down the middle of them. To the east of these snow-capped mountains, rain forests cover the land. Ecuador grows and sells a lot of bananas. Peru is one of the world's leading fishing countries.

Bolivia is different from Ecuador and Peru. It is landlocked. This means it is surrounded by land and is not next to an ocean. The Andes Mountains spread across the western border of Bolivia. This country is one of the poorest in South America. Many Indians make these three countries their home. You can hear their languages and music in small Andean villages.

■ Quito
▲ Cotopaxi Volcano
Ambato
ECUADOR
Guayaquil
▲ Sangay Volcano
Cuenca

Chiclayo

Trujillo

PACIFIC

OCEAN

If you travel thrrough the Andes Mountains, you should get yourself a llama. A llama is a relative of the camel. It can carry about 130 pounds for nearly 20 miles. But be careful. If your llama's load is too heavy, it will lie down and refuse to move.

Andean Music

Music has been important to the people of Andean South America for hundreds of years. Long ago, people called the Incas lived in the Andes Mountains. They played many instruments. They made flutes and trumpets from wood and drums from hollow logs covered with animal skin. Today the music they created is called Andean music. It is named for the Andes Mountains.

Today's Andean music still has a sound similar to that of long ago. Over the years it has become a mixture of native, Spanish, and African music. It has become popular in many parts of the world.

Lima is the capital and largest city of Peru. It lies in western Peru, about ten miles from the Pacific Ocean. Lima was the center of government when Spain ruled Peru from the 1530s to the early 1800s. Many of the mansions built then still stand today.

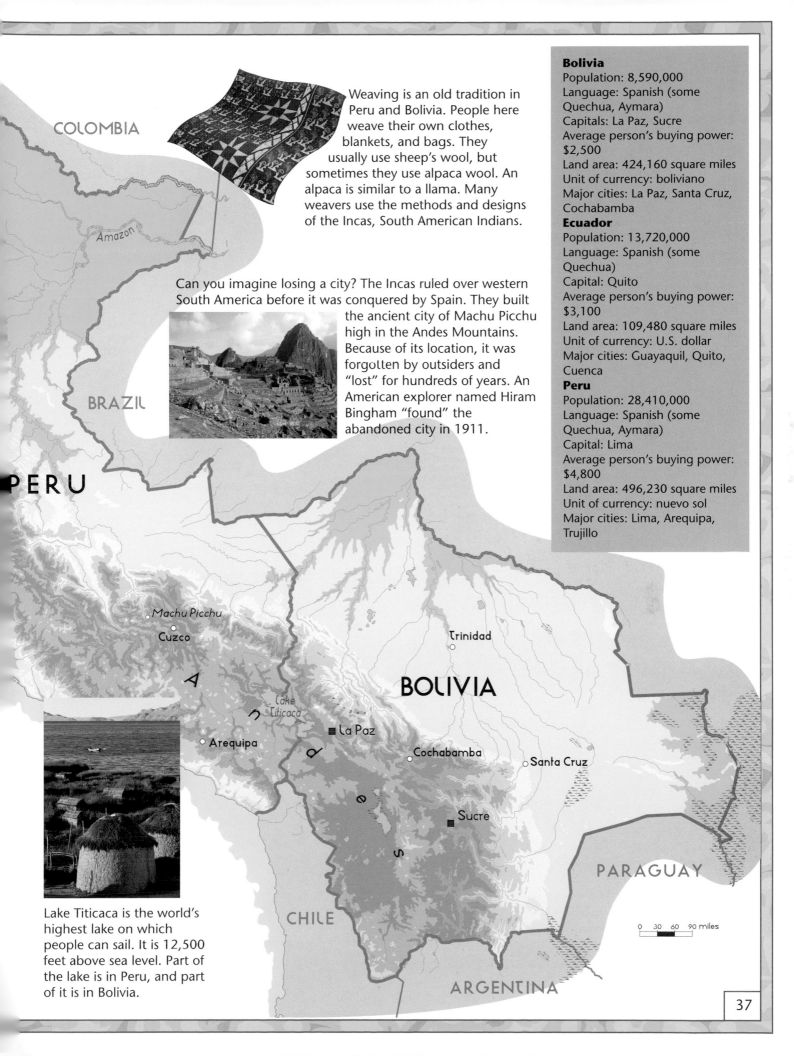

Weaving is an old tradition in Peru and Bolivia. People here weave their own clothes, blankets, and bags. They usually use sheep's wool, but sometimes they use alpaca wool. An alpaca is similar to a llama. Many weavers use the methods and designs of the Incas, South American Indians.

Can you imagine losing a city? The Incas ruled over western South America before it was conquered by Spain. They built the ancient city of Machu Picchu high in the Andes Mountains. Because of its location, it was forgotten by outsiders and "lost" for hundreds of years. An American explorer named Hiram Bingham "found" the abandoned city in 1911.

Bolivia
Population: 8,590,000
Language: Spanish (some Quechua, Aymara)
Capitals: La Paz, Sucre
Average person's buying power: $2,500
Land area: 424,160 square miles
Unit of currency: boliviano
Major cities: La Paz, Santa Cruz, Cochabamba

Ecuador
Population: 13,720,000
Language: Spanish (some Quechua)
Capital: Quito
Average person's buying power: $3,100
Land area: 109,480 square miles
Unit of currency: U.S. dollar
Major cities: Guayaquil, Quito, Cuenca

Peru
Population: 28,410,000
Language: Spanish (some Quechua, Aymara)
Capital: Lima
Average person's buying power: $4,800
Land area: 496,230 square miles
Unit of currency: nuevo sol
Major cities: Lima, Arequipa, Trujillo

Lake Titicaca is the world's highest lake on which people can sail. It is 12,500 feet above sea level. Part of the lake is in Peru, and part of it is in Bolivia.

0   30   60   90 miles

Brazil

Brazil is the biggest country in South America. It is so big, it takes up almost half of the entire continent. About the same number of people live here as in all the other countries of South America combined. This country is also home to the world's largest rain forest and second-longest river. The Amazon River helps supply the rain forest with water. Sadly, the rain forests are quickly disappearing. This is because more and more people are coming to the rain forest to live. They are clearing the land for farms. Many plants and animals can be found only in the forest. They are disappearing with the trees. Many native South American forest cultures are also disappearing.

Are you ready to dance? Samba and bossa nova are popular kinds of music in Brazil. Samba uses a wide variety of drums and other percussion instruments. Bossa nova is a dance music. It combines the rhythm of samba with jazz music.

PERU

0 60 120 180 miles

The Amazon River and the Rain Forests

The Amazon River is the second-longest river in the world. It flows for 4,000 miles. You could walk from New York to San Francisco and still not travel its length. In some places, the Amazon is 35 miles wide. The river empties into the Atlantic Ocean. More water flows through the Amazon than through any other river on earth.

Those muddy waters flow through Brazil's rain forests, which cover one-third of the country. They are home to hundreds of thousands of animals and plants. Several native peoples still live in the forest as well. The Yanomamo people live in villages on the border of Brazil and Venezuela.

The earth beneath Brazil is rich with minerals. If you went to the mines in Brazil, you might find metals such as iron ore, gold, bauxite, manganese, nickel, platinum, tin, and uranium. You could also find quartz crystals, amethysts, and diamonds. Some people make money by mining and processing these minerals.

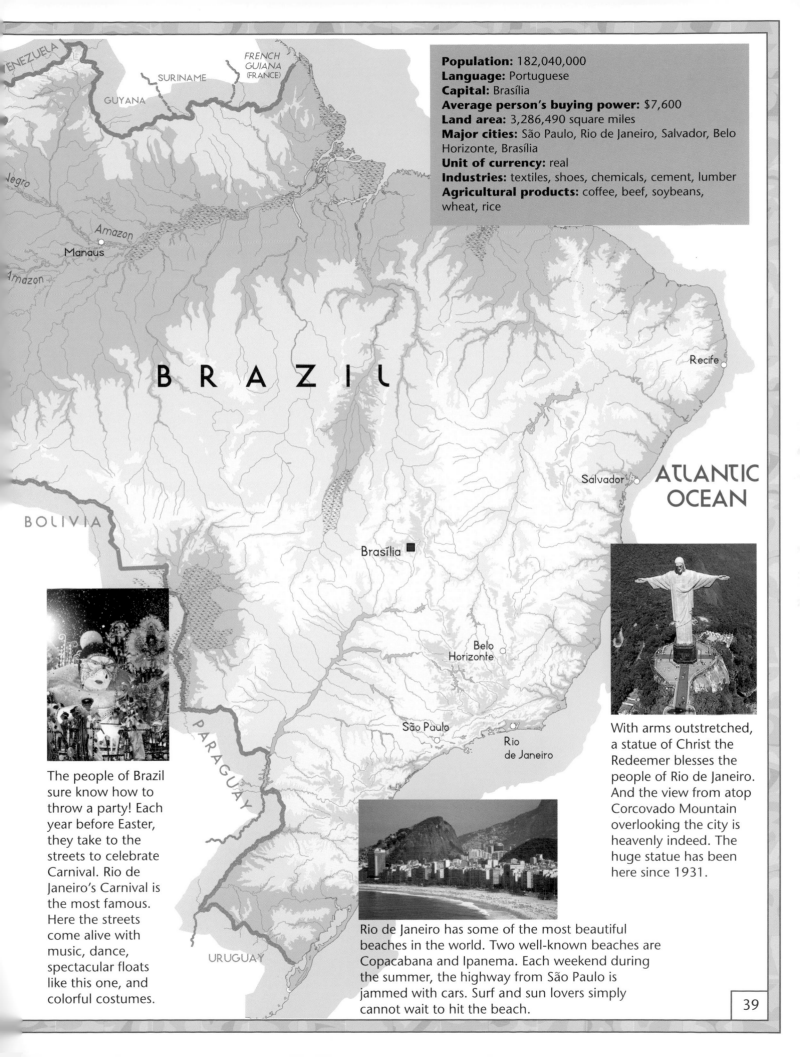

Population: 182,040,000
Language: Portuguese
Capital: Brasília
Average person's buying power: $7,600
Land area: 3,286,490 square miles
Major cities: São Paulo, Rio de Janeiro, Salvador, Belo Horizonte, Brasília
Unit of currency: real
Industries: textiles, shoes, chemicals, cement, lumber
Agricultural products: coffee, beef, soybeans, wheat, rice

VENEZUELA
SURINAME
FRENCH GUIANA (FRANCE)
GUYANA
Negro
Amazon
Manaus
Amazon
BOLIVIA
BRAZIL
Recife
Salvador
ATLANTIC OCEAN
Brasília
Belo Horizonte
PARAGUAY
São Paulo
Rio de Janeiro
URUGUAY

The people of Brazil sure know how to throw a party! Each year before Easter, they take to the streets to celebrate Carnival. Rio de Janeiro's Carnival is the most famous. Here the streets come alive with music, dance, spectacular floats like this one, and colorful costumes.

With arms outstretched, a statue of Christ the Redeemer blesses the people of Rio de Janeiro. And the view from atop Corcovado Mountain overlooking the city is heavenly indeed. The huge statue has been here since 1931.

Rio de Janeiro has some of the most beautiful beaches in the world. Two well-known beaches are Copacabana and Ipanema. Each weekend during the summer, the highway from São Paulo is jammed with cars. Surf and sun lovers simply cannot wait to hit the beach.

Southern Cone

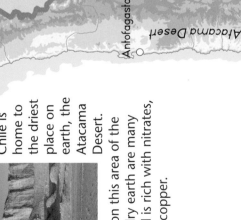

Montevideo is the capital of Uruguay. It is also the country's largest city. The city's name came from something a Portuguese sailor once said. When he spotted the Cerro, a hill that stands near the city, he called out, "Monte vide eu!" That means "I see a hill!"

Northern Chile is home to the driest place on earth, the Atacama Desert.

Rain just doesn't fall on this area of the world. Beneath this dry earth are many minerals. The ground is rich with nitrates, iodine, iron ore, and copper.

Fruit grows well in the center of Chile. It grows so well that Chile sells a lot of fresh fruit to other countries. This fruit includes grapes, apples, peaches, pears, oranges, lemons, and limes.

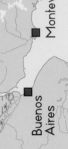

BRAZIL

PARAGUAY

Concepción
Ciudad del Este
Villarrica
Asunción
Paraguay
Encarnación
Paraná

URUGUAY

Salto
Paysandú
Montevideo

Buenos Aires
Rosario
Paraná

Córdoba

ARGENTINA

BOLIVIA

Antofagasta
Atacama Desert
Cerro del Potro
CHILE

Viña del Mar
Valparaíso
Santiago

Concepción

PACIFIC OCEAN

0 60 120 180 miles

Buenos Aires is Argentina's capital and largest city. It lies in eastern Argentina on a muddy bay called the Rio de la Plata. The world's widest street, Avenida Nueve de Julio, is here. This street is 425 feet wide! Its name means Ninth of July Avenue. Argentina became independent from Spain on July 9, 1816.

Gauchos on the Pampas

If you see gauchos galloping across wide-open plains, you are probably in Argentina! Gauchos are the cowboys of this country. They are skilled at riding horses. They use their skill to herd cattle on treeless grasslands. These great plains in the northern half of Argentina and in Uruguay are called the Pampas. Gauchos have become folk heroes in Argentina. Many poems and stories have been written about them.

ATLANTIC OCEAN

P a t a g o n i a

Tierra Del Fuego

The area called Patagonia is in Argentina's extreme south. It covers more than one-fourth of the country. A cold, dry wind makes life very hard, so few people live here. You won't see a lot of people in Patagonia, but you will see sheep! Raising sheep is the region's main business. You will also see quite a few penguins.

Argentina
Population: 38,750,000
Language: Spanish
Capital: Buenos Aires
Average person's buying power: $10,200
Land area: 1,068,300 square miles
Unit of currency: Argentine peso
Major cities: Buenos Aires, Córdoba, Rosario

Chile
Population: 15,670,000
Language: Spanish (some English)
Capital: Santiago
Average person's buying power: $10,000
Land area: 292,260 square miles
Unit of currency: Chilean peso
Major cities: Santiago, Viña del Mar, Antofagasta, Valparaíso

Paraguay
Population: 6,040,000
Language: Spanish (some Guarani)
Capital: Asunción
Average person's buying power: $4,200
Land area: 157,050 square miles
Unit of currency: guarani
Major cities: Asunción, Ciudad del Este

Uruguay
Population: 3,420,000
Language: Spanish
Capital: Montevideo
Average person's buying power: $7,800
Land area: 68,040 square miles
Unit of currency: Uruguayan peso
Major cities: Montevideo, Salto, Paysandú

At the southern end of South America lie Chile, Argentina, Uruguay, and Paraguay. Together, they make a sort of cone shape. The Andes Mountains stretch down the western edge of this area. Chile, a long and narrow country, is sandwiched between these mountains and the Pacific Ocean. It is more than 20 times as long as it is wide.

Grassy, rolling plains cover Argentina and Uruguay. Huge herds of cows and sheep graze on the grass here. Argentina alone has more than 50 million cows! The river Paraguay divides Paraguay. Almost the entire population lives in the eastern half of the country.

Europe

Europe is a small continent, but it has had a big effect on world history. Many ideas from science and art to religion and politics have come from the minds of Europeans.

Australia is the only continent that is smaller than Europe. However, about one-eighth of the world's population lives in Europe.

Europe and Asia belong to the same mass of land. Together the two continents are often called Eurasia. They are separated by their histories and different ways of life. The dividing line between them runs along the Ural Mountains and the Black Sea. The Russian Federation and Turkey are in Europe and Asia. Europe is bounded by the Arctic and Atlantic Oceans in the north and west and the Mediterranean Sea in the south.

The landscape of Europe is quite varied. Some countries are very flat. Others are covered with huge forests. Still others lie in the shadow of towering mountain ranges.

Europe has 44 countries. They range in size from the Russian Federation, which is sometimes called Russia and is the largest country in the world, to the Holy See, which is the smallest.

Highest point: Mount Elbrus (Russia), 18,510 feet

Lowest point: Caspian Sea (Russia), 92 feet below sea level

Major rivers: Volga (Russia) 2,290 miles; Danube (Germany, Austria, Slovakia, Hungary, Croatia, Serbia and Montenegro, Romania, Bulgaria), 1,776 miles; Dnieper (Russia, Belarus, Ukraine) 1,420 miles; Rhine (Switzerland, Germany, Netherlands), 820 miles

Biggest lakes: Lake Ladoga (Russia), 6,835 square miles; Lake Onega (Russia), 3,720 square miles; Lake Vanern (Sweden), 2,156 square miles

Major mountains: Mount Elbrus (Russia),

18,510 feet; Mont Blanc (France, Italy), 15,771 feet; Monte Rosa (Italy), 15,203

Total land area: 3,837,080 square miles

Total population: 698,000,000

Largest country (area): Russia, 6,592,800 square miles (Russia is in Europe and Asia; area of European Russia is about 1,600,000 square miles)

Smallest country (area): Holy See (Vatican City), 0.17 square mile

Largest country (population): Russia, 144,530,000 (Russia is in Europe and Asia; population of European Russia is about 113,000,000)

Smallest country (population): Holy See (Vatican City), 900

ARCTIC OCEAN

NORWEGIAN
SEA

BARENTS
SEA

WHITE SEA

NORWAY

SWEDEN

FINLAND

Baltic Sea

Ural Mountains

ESTONIA

LATVIA

DENMARK

NORTH
SEA

LITHUANIA

RUSSIAN FED.

RUSSIAN FEDERATION

BELARUS

NETHERLANDS

GERMANY

POLAND

BELGIUM

LUXEMBOURG

LIECHTENSTEIN

CZECH REPUBLIC

UKRAINE

ASIA

SLOVAKIA

AUSTRIA

HUNGARY

MOLDOVA

SWITZERLAND

SLOVENIA

CROATIA

ROMANIA

FRANCE

ITALY

SAN
MARINO

BOSNIA AND
HERZEGOVINA

SERBIA AND
MONTENEGRO

MONACO

BULGARIA

BLACK SEA

CASPIAN SEA

HOLY
SEE

MACEDONIA

ALBANIA

TURKEY

MALTA

GREECE

ASIA

AEGEAN
SEA

MEDITERRANEAN SEA

AFRICA

0   250   500   750 miles

United Kingdom

This country's full name is United Kingdom of Great Britain and Northern Ireland. Some people call it the United Kingdom or the UK. Others call it Great Britain. But no matter what you call it, this country includes England, Scotland, Wales, and Northern Ireland. In the past, the British empire controlled nearly one-fourth of the land on earth. Many countries, such as the United States, Canada, India, Australia, and Ireland, were part of the empire before they gained independence.

England, Scotland, and Wales are on the island of Great Britain. Ireland is another island. Most of it is the country of Ireland, but the northeast corner, called Northern Ireland, is separate. This corner is part of the UK.

For hundreds of years, a lake in Scotland has been rumored to be the home of a monster! Loch Ness is about 23 miles long. Many people have reported seeing a large, long-necked monster in its waters, but scientists say there is nothing there. People have named the Loch Ness monster Nessie.

Bagpipes and tartans are very Scottish. To play the bagpipes, you blow through a mouthpiece into a bag that has one or more pipes. At the same time, you squeeze the bag, and a sound comes out. Tartan is a design like plaid. Each Scottish family, or clan, has its own tartan design.

NORTH
SEA

Loch Ness

Scotland

Edinburgh

Glasgow

Belfast

ATLANTIC

OCEAN

Northern Ireland

IRELAND

IRISH SEA

UNITED KINGDOM

England

Wales

Leeds

Sheffield

Manchester

Liverpool

Birmingham

Stratford-upon-Avon

Cardiff

London

CELTIC SEA

ENGLISH CHANNEL

0 15 30 45 miles

Union Jack is the name sometimes used for the flag of the United Kingdom. It is a combination of England's, Scotland's, and Ireland's emblems. England's emblem is a red cross on a white background. Scotland's is a white X on blue. Ireland's is a red X on white. Can you see all three in the Union Jack?

Sports

Want to play a game of cricket? How about rounders or rugby? You don't know how to play these games? Well, then, you are definitely not from the United Kingdom!

The people of the UK are big sports fans. Their favorite sport is what Americans call soccer. They call it football. Cricket is a little bit like baseball. Two teams play the game with bats and a ball. It has been popular for hundreds of years. Another game like baseball is rounders. American baseball started as this game. Rugby, shown below, is a very rough sport. It is similar to American football.

William Shakespeare is the most famous writer of English-language plays in the world. He wrote *Romeo and Juliet*, *Hamlet*, and many others. He was born more than 400 years ago in Stratford-upon-Avon, one of the oldest towns in England. Today, his plays are performed all over the world.

Population: 60,100,000
Language: English (some Welsh, Scottish, Gaelic)
Capital: London
Average person's buying power: $25,300
Land area: 94,530 square miles
Unit of currency: British pound
Major cities: London, Birmingham, Leeds, Glasgow, Sheffield
Industries: machine tools, electric power equipment, railroad equipment, shipbuilding, aircraft
Agricultural products: cereals, cattle, fish, potatoes, sheep

Want to set your watch? Look to the clock tower in the Houses of Parliament in London. And listen to Big Ben, the giant bell in the clock. Some people think the clock and clock tower are also named Big Ben, but it is only the name of the bell.

They stand as still as statues outside Buckingham Palace in London. They wear bright red coats and tall, furry black hats. But all at once, they come to life. It's the changing of the guard! This ceremony occurs frequently. Buckingham Palace is the home of the British royal family.

Ireland

Ireland is an island in the Atlantic Ocean. The Republic of Ireland shares it with the UK. The republic is often simply called Ireland. It takes up most of the land.

The center of Ireland is covered with lowlands. Much of this area is used for farming. There are also many meadows and pastures. Many people think of the color green when they think of Ireland because there is so much grass here! No matter where you stand in Ireland, you are never more than 70 miles from the ocean. Ireland is also a country that has many legends.

The Irish countryside is a patchwork of stone walls. There are many thousands of miles of stone wall in Ireland. Farmers built these walls a long time ago. Each family had its own way of building, so you can see different styles of stone walls.

SCOTLAND
UNITED KINGDOM

North Channel

NORTHERN IRELAND (UK)

ATLANTIC OCEAN

0   12   24   36 miles

In Ireland many houses have a brightly painted front door. This may be because the weather here is often dreary. Or it may be due to the bleakness of stone and cement. Perhaps it's for both reasons. But if you visit Ireland, expect to see doors of many colors.

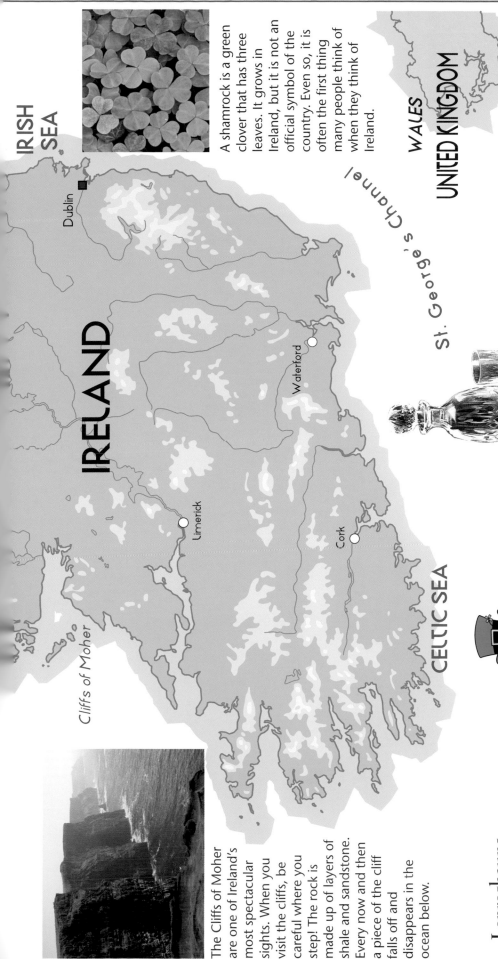

A shamrock is a green clover that has three leaves. It grows in Ireland, but it is not an official symbol of the country. Even so, it is often the first thing many people think of when they think of Ireland.

WALES

UNITED KINGDOM

Population: 3,930,000
Language: English (some Gaelic)
Capital: Dublin
Average person's buying power: $30,500
Land area: 27,140 square miles
Unit of currency: euro
Major cities: Dublin, Cork, Limerick
Industries: food products, textiles, chemicals, pharmaceuticals, software
Agricultural products: turnips, barley, potatoes, beef, dairy products

Dublin

IRELAND

Waterford

St. George's Channel

Limerick

Cork

Cliffs of Moher

CELTIC SEA

Ireland is famous for crystals and linen fabrics. Crystal is a type of glass. It can be shaped into glasses, vases, and dishes. Waterford, Ireland, is known worldwide for its crystal. Linen is the yarn made from the flax plant. Irish weavers use the yarn to create beautiful linen fabrics.

The Cliffs of Moher are one of Ireland's most spectacular sights. When you visit the cliffs, be careful where you step! The rock is made up of layers of shale and sandstone. Every now and then a piece of the cliff falls off and disappears in the ocean below.

Leprechauns

When you think of Ireland, do you think of leprechauns? Leprechauns are Irish fairies. They are a popular symbol of this European country.

Leprechauns look like tiny men. According to legend, they are shoemakers. Legends also claim leprechauns have a hidden pot of gold. It is said that you can find a leprechaun by listening for his shoemaker's hammer. If you catch him, you can force him to tell you where he's hidden his gold.

Northern Europe

Parts of Northern Europe reach far north, beyond the Arctic Circle. The people here must brave some very cold weather. Their winter days are long and dark. In the southern areas of Northern Europe, however, the weather is warmer, especially in summer.

In Sweden and Norway, mountains and forests cover much of the land. Very little farming takes place in the north. But almost all of Denmark is used for farming. Thousands of lakes are scattered all over Finland, Estonia, Latvia, and Lithuania.

Iceland is an island in the North Atlantic Ocean. Some parts of Iceland are so similar to the surface of the moon that astronauts trained here for moon landings.

You'd better bring plenty of warm clothes to Sweden's Icehotel. Its beds are ice blocks covered with reindeer skins. You can eat and drink from ice plates and ice glasses. The hotel is only open during the winter. Every spring it melts, so it has to be built all over again each November.

The Sami people live in parts of Norway, Sweden, and Finland called Lapland. Some Sami herd reindeer. They eat and sell reindeer meat, drink reindeer milk, and use reindeer skin for clothing. Traditional Sami clothing is warm and colorful!

BARENTS SEA

RUSSIA

Lapland

FINLAND

Gulf of Bothnia

SWEDEN

Helsinki

NORWEGIAN SEA

0 25 50 75 miles

Map Labels

RUSSIA · LATVIA · BELARUS · ESTONIA · LITHUANIA

Vilnius · Riga · Gulf of Riga

RUSSIA · POLAND · GERMANY · DENMARK · Copenhagen

BALTIC SEA · NORTH SEA

Stockholm · Oslo

GREENLAND SEA · Denmark Strait · ICELAND · Reykjavik · ATLANTIC OCEAN

0   30   60 miles

Iceland is sometimes called the land of fire and ice. It got this name because huge sheets of ice called glaciers lie next to steaming hot springs, geysers, and volcanoes. Some of the landscape here looks like nowhere else on earth.

With so much coastline

With so much coastline, it is no wonder fishing is important to this part of the world. The fish here include cod, herring, and haddock. After the fish is caught, most of it is dried, salted, or quick-frozen for sale to other countries.

Fjords

The entire coastline of Norway looks like a jagged knife. The many inlets along the coast are called fjords. Fjords are narrow bays in which the ocean cuts into the land between steep cliffs. Fjords can be much deeper than you might expect. Norway's deepest fjord, Sognefjord, is also its longest. It is about 125 miles long and more than 4,000 feet deep. Glaciers carved these fjords thousands of years ago during the ice ages.

Did you know that reindeer really do exist? They roam parts of Northern Europe. Reindeer are a type of deer. They have large antlers and big, wide hoofs. They also have a heavy coat of fur. Some people use reindeer to pull heavy loads, such as sleighs!

Country Facts

Denmark
Population: 5,390,000
Language: Danish (some Faroese)
Capital: Copenhagen
Average person's buying power: $29,000

Estonia
Population: 1,410,000
Language: Estonian (some Russian)
Capital: Tallinn
Average person's buying power: $10,900

Finland
Population: 5,200,000
Languages: Finnish (some Swedish)
Capital: Helsinki
Average person's buying power: $26,200

Iceland
Population: 290,000
Language: Icelandic
Capital: Reykjavik
Average person's buying power: $25,000

Latvia
Population: 2,350,000
Language: Latvian (some Russian)
Capital: Riga
Average person's buying power: $8,300

Lithuania
Population: 3,600,000
Language: Lithuanian
Capital: Vilnius
Average person's buying power: $8,400

Norway
Population: 4,550,000
Language: Norwegian
Capital: Oslo
Average person's buying power: $31,800

Sweden
Population: 8,880,000
Language: Swedish
Capital: Stockholm
Average person's buying power: $25,400

Germany

Germany is divided into 16 federal states with names such as Bavaria, Saxony, and Schleswig-Holstein. Each of these regions has its own way of life, and the people speak German in their own unique way.

The North Sea and the Baltic Sea give Germany a bit of coastline in the north. The Rhine River snakes through the valleys to the west. Germany's highest mountains, the Bavarian Alps, tower over the land in the south.

For almost half of the 20th century, Germany was divided into two countries: East Germany and West Germany. On October 3, 1990, history was made. These two countries came together as a single nation again.

Imagine your town is divided by a big wall. You are not allowed to cross it or see anyone on the other side. When Germany was two countries, its capital, Berlin, was divided by the Berlin Wall. In 1989 the wall came down. Berlin was still in two different countries, but people could come and go again as they pleased!

Population: 82,400,000
Language: German
Capital: Berlin
Average person's buying power: $26,600
Land area: 137,850 square miles
Unit of currency: euro
Major cities: Berlin, Hamburg, Munich, Cologne
Industries: iron, steel, coal, shipbuilding, textiles
Agricultural products: potatoes, wheat, barley, cattle, pigs

POLAND

BALTIC SEA

Berlin

DENMARK

Elbe

Hamburg

Hanover

NORTH SEA

NETHERLANDS

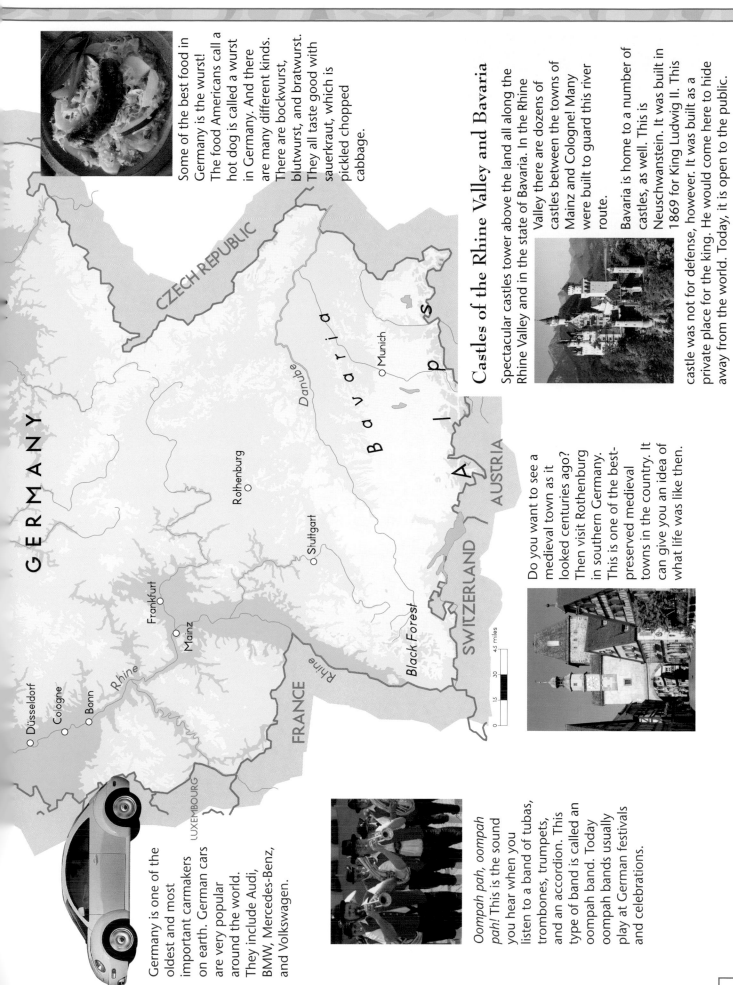

Some of the best food in Germany is the wurst! The food Americans call a hot dog is called a wurst in Germany. And there are many different kinds. There are bockwurst, blutwurst, and bratwurst. They all taste good with sauerkraut, which is pickled chopped cabbage.

Castles of the Rhine Valley and Bavaria

Spectacular castles tower above the land all along the Rhine Valley and in the state of Bavaria. In the Rhine Valley there are dozens of castles between the towns of Mainz and Cologne! Many were built to guard this river route.

Bavaria is home to a number of castles, as well. This is Neuschwanstein. It was built in 1869 for King Ludwig II. This castle was not for defense, however. It was built as a private place for the king. He would come here to hide away from the world. Today, it is open to the public.

Do you want to see a medieval town as it looked centuries ago? Then visit Rothenburg in southern Germany. This is one of the best-preserved medieval towns in the country. It can give you an idea of what life was like then.

Oompah pah, oompah pah! This is the sound you hear when you listen to a band of tubas, trombones, trumpets, and an accordion. This type of band is called an oompah band. Today oompah bands usually play at German festivals and celebrations.

Germany is one of the oldest and most important carmakers on earth. German cars are very popular around the world. They include Audi, BMW, Mercedes-Benz, and Volkswagen.

GERMANY

CZECH REPUBLIC

Danube

Bavaria

Munich

Alps

Rothenburg

Stuttgart

AUSTRIA

Frankfurt

Mainz

SWITZERLAND

Rhine

Black Forest

Düsseldorf

Cologne

Bonn

Rhine

FRANCE

LUXEMBOURG

0   15   30   45 miles

51

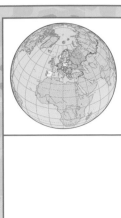

Low Countries

What do you get when you combine the first few letters of the names *Belgium*, *Netherlands*, and *Luxembourg?* You get *Benelux*. This is the name sometimes used for this area of Europe.

These three countries are also sometimes called the Low Countries. This is because most of their land is low and flat. Much of Netherlands is below sea level and was once covered by water. While most of the land in Belgium and Luxembourg is flat, the Ardennes hills stretch across parts of both countries.

The Low Countries are among Europe's richest and most developed countries.

Amsterdam is a city full of canals. This capital city was built on marshy land just below sea level. More than 100 canals crisscross the city to help drain the land. Because there is so much water, many people travel around the city in boats.

There are many reminders that the Netherlands is waterlogged. Windmills are a common sight. They once powered pumps for draining flooded fields. Dikes are like dams. They keep the land dry. And in spring, the fields are ablaze with the color of tulips. These flowers are big business here.

Wouldn't you like to visit the Peace Palace in "Peace City"? It sounds like a made-up place. But it's not. The Hague is called "Peace City." The headquarters of the International Court of Justice is in the Peace Palace. This court helps to settle arguments between countries.

NORTH SEA

NETHERLANDS

Amsterdam

The Hague

Delft

Rotterdam

Rhine

0 10 20 30 miles

If your fine china is marked with a *D*, you know it came from the Netherlands! Pottery is made throughout this country. But the most well-known ceramics are made in the village of Delft. Delftware is some of the finest porcelain in the world.

Belgium
Population: 10,290,000
Languages: Dutch, French, German
Capital: Brussels
Average person's buying power: $29,000
Land area: 11,780 square miles
Unit of currency: euro
Major cities: Brussels, Antwerp

Luxembourg
Population: 460,000
Languages: Luxembourgish, German, French
Capital: Luxembourg
Average person's buying power: $44,000
Land area: 1,000 square miles
Unit of currency: euro
Major city: Luxembourg

Netherlands
Population: 16,160,000
Language: Dutch
Capitals: Amsterdam, The Hague
Average person's buying power: $26,900
Land area: 16,030 square miles
Unit of currency: euro
Major cities: Amsterdam, Rotterdam, The Hague

The flat land of the Low Countries is perfect for riding bikes. On weekends, bicyclists of all ages ride through the streets and countryside. But bicycles are not just for fun. They are also used instead of cars for transportation.

The Europoort is one of the biggest and busiest seaports in the world. Ships loaded with goods move in and out of the port, which lies near the city of Rotterdam where the Rhine River flows into the North Sea. The port handles many goods that are headed to and from countries in the European Union.

European Union

Wouldn't it be nice if all the countries in the world could get along and work together? Well, there is a group of countries that have agreed to try to do just that. The countries in the European Union (EU) have made an agreement to help each other in certain areas, such as business. Most countries in the EU use the same currency, the euro. The EU parliament sometimes meets in this building in Brussels.

The EU has 25 members: Austria, Belgium, Cyprus, the Czech Republic, Denmark, Estonia, Finland, France, Germany, Greece, Hungary, Ireland, Italy, Latvia, Lithuania, Luxembourg, Malta, Netherlands, Poland, Portugal, Slovakia, Slovenia, Spain, Sweden, and the United Kingdom.

France

Brittany

Nantes

The French countryside is covered with farmland. France has a very successful farming industry. For example, the northern plains are covered in fields of wheat and sugar beets. Grapes dot the central and southern regions.

ATLANTIC

OCEAN

Bordea

0   20   30   60 miles

SPAIN

Py

rance has more land than any other country in Western Europe. Because it is so large, France has a large variety of terrain. The Alps form the border between France and Italy at the southeastern corner. Another mountain range, the Pyrénées, forms the border with Spain in the southwest. Beaches stretch along the Mediterranean Sea to the south, and villages dot the Atlantic coast to the northwest.

Monaco is one of the smallest countries in the world. Its area is less than one square mile. It lies on the French Riviera, which borders the Mediterranean Sea. France borders Monaco on the other three sides.

Can you guess why the French flag is nicknamed *tricolor?* Count the number of colors on the flag. There are three, right? Well, the prefix *tri-* means *three!* Hundreds of years ago, blue and red were the colors of Paris, and white was the color of the king.

Trains

You're in Paris, and you want to get someplace fast. Should you take a cab or a car? No way! Hop a train.

The train system in France focuses on speed. In 1981, the country launched *Train à Grande Vitesse (TGV)*. This is French for high-speed train. France's high-speed trains were designed to carry passengers from Paris to other French cities at lightning speed. The trains can move up to 186 miles per hour! Today there are three

major rail lines that travel out of Paris. The most recent one connects Paris to Belgium and Britain.

France
Population: 60,190,000
Language: French (some Breton)
Capital: Paris
Average person's buying power: $25,700
Land area: 211,210 square miles
Unit of currency: euro
Major cities: Paris, Marseille, Lyon, Toulouse
Industries: machinery, chemicals, automobiles, textiles, tourism
Agricultural products: wheat, cereals, sugar beets, beef, fish
Monaco
Population: 32,000
Languages: French, English, Italian
Capital: Monaco
Average person's buying power: $27,000

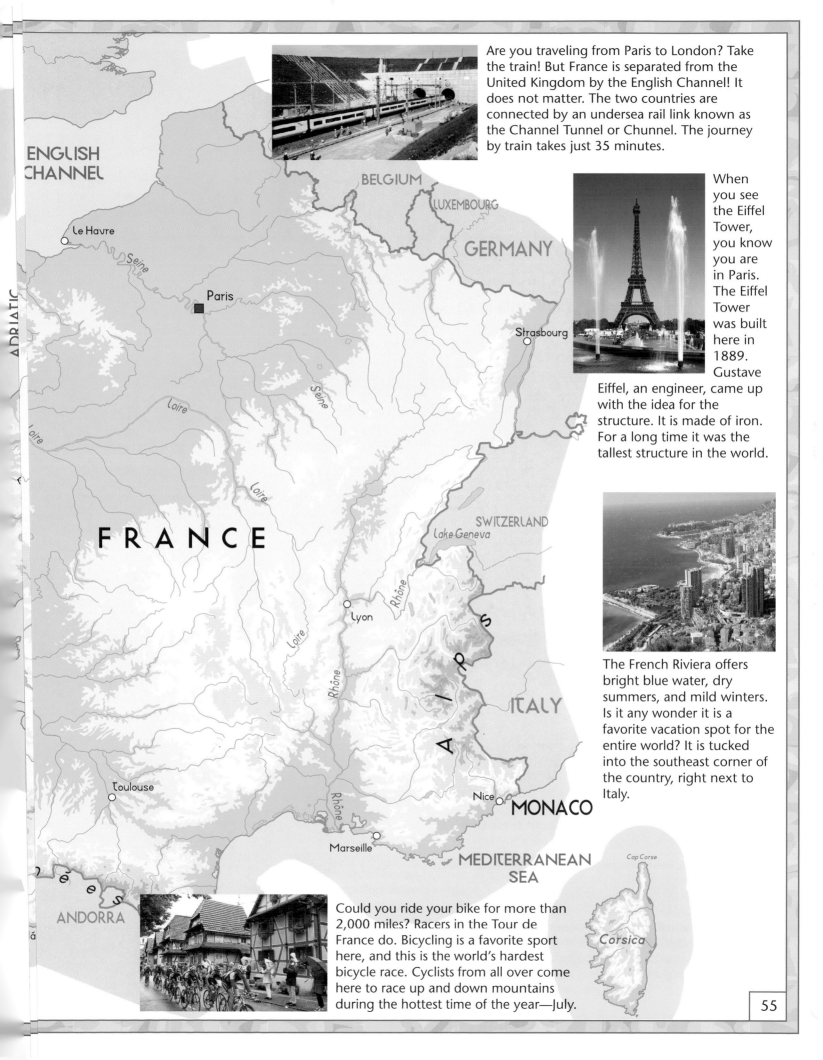

Are you traveling from Paris to London? Take the train! But France is separated from the United Kingdom by the English Channel! It does not matter. The two countries are connected by an undersea rail link known as the Channel Tunnel or Chunnel. The journey by train takes just 35 minutes.

When you see the Eiffel Tower, you know you are in Paris. The Eiffel Tower was built here in 1889. Gustave Eiffel, an engineer, came up with the idea for the structure. It is made of iron. For a long time it was the tallest structure in the world.

The French Riviera offers bright blue water, dry summers, and mild winters. Is it any wonder it is a favorite vacation spot for the entire world? It is tucked into the southeast corner of the country, right next to Italy.

Could you ride your bike for more than 2,000 miles? Racers in the Tour de France do. Bicycling is a favorite sport here, and this is the world's hardest bicycle race. Cyclists from all over come here to race up and down mountains during the hottest time of the year—July.

ENGLISH CHANNEL

ADRIATIC

Le Havre

Seine

BELGIUM

LUXEMBOURG

GERMANY

Paris

Strasbourg

Seine

Loire

Loire

Loire

FRANCE

SWITZERLAND

Lake Geneva

Rhône

Rhône

Lyon

ALPS

ITALY

Rhône

Toulouse

Nice

MONACO

Marseille

MEDITERRANEAN SEA

Cap Corse

ANDORRA

Corsica

Switzerland and Austria

Austria and Switzerland are surrounded by land. Neither sits on a body of water. However, both have spectacular mountain scenery. The Alps stretch across both of these countries.

Switzerland is a land of peace. It has not been at war with another country since 1814. This is why people from all over the world put their money into Swiss banks. They know their money will be safe here.

Many farms and businesses operate on Austria's northeastern lowlands. Europe's second-longest river, the Danube, snakes through here. Nearly one-fifth of Austria's people live in the capital city, Vienna. Liechtenstein is a tiny country between Switzerland and Austria.

Liechtenstein is a tiny country that lies between Austria and Switzerland. It is a land of fairy-tale castles. The prince of Liechtenstein lives in one of these castles. It is in Vaduz, the capital.

When you think of Switzerland, you probably picture mountains. And there is no other mountain quite like the Matterhorn. This famous mountain has a jagged peak. It calls out to mountain climbers: "Are you brave enough to climb me?" Many climbers have tried, and many have failed.

Austria
Population: 8,190,000
Language: German
Capital: Vienna
Average person's buying power: $27,700
Land area: 32,380 square miles
Unit of currency: euro
Major cities: Vienna, Graz, Linz
Industries: construction, machinery, vehicles and parts, food, chemicals
Agricultural products: grains, potatoes, dairy, cattle, lumber
Switzerland
Population: 7,320,000
Languages: German, French, Italian, Romansch

Capital: Bern
Average person's buying power: $31,700
Land area: 15,940 square miles
Unit of currency: Swiss franc
Major cities: Zurich, Basel, Geneva
Industries: machinery, chemicals, watches, textiles, precision instruments
Agricultural products: grains, fruits, vegetables, meat, eggs
Liechtenstein
Population: 35,000
Language: German
Capital: Vaduz
Average person's buying power: $25,000

Could you perform music for an empress? How nervous would you be? That is what Wolfgang Amadeus Mozart did. He was only six years old when he went on tour to play the piano. Mozart was born in Salzburg, Austria, in 1756. He became one of the world's greatest writers of music.

The Danube River is Austria's largest river. If you were to travel the Danube, you would pass through Austria's largest cities, such as Vienna. Vienna is Austria's capital and biggest city. It was once a route for trade between western and central Europe. This was important to Vienna's early growth as a city.

CZECH REPUBLIC

SLOVAKIA

Danube Linz Danube ■ Vienna

0 15 30 45 miles

Salzburg

GERMANY

AUSTRIA

HUNGARY

Innsbruck l p s Graz

ITALY

SLOVENIA

CROATIA

Switzerland is famous for milk and cheese. So you know what that means—cows! There are a lot of cows in Switzerland! And from their milk, the Swiss make the world's tastiest chocolate. They also make Swiss cheese. This is the cheese with all the holes.

It's hard to hear in the mountains. That is why the alphorn came about. It is a gigantic horn used to call in cattle from the mountains. People dress in traditional clothing for special festivals. Men and boys wear lederhosen, which are leather shorts with suspenders. Women and girls wear dirndls, or mountain-style jumpers.

The Alps

The Alps are the largest group of mountains in Europe. This mountain range covers much of Switzerland and Austria. It also stretches into Germany, France, and Italy. The Alps are very tall and rugged. Some peaks are covered with snow almost year-round.

The Alps have glaciers, which are slow-moving sheets of ice. They create ice caves in the mountains. As the glaciers melt, the water makes many waterfalls.

People visit the Alps to see the beautiful scenery and enjoy many winter sports. Skiing, bobsledding, and tobogganing are all popular. When the snow melts, the Alps are covered with tall grasses and wildflowers.

Greece

MACEDONIA

ADRIATIC SEA

ALBANIA

ITALY

IONIAN SEA

Thessaloniki

Mount Olympus

GREECE

0   20   40   60 miles

More than 2,500 years ago, Greece was the center of civilization. It was home to great artists, writers, and thinkers. In those days, Greece controlled much of the land around the current borders. Today magnificent ruins stand as reminders of the country's past.

Greece is a great vacation spot. This small country has sunny weather and beautiful scenery. Rugged mountains cover much of the land. Rock islands dot the Aegean Sea near the mainland. Ferries carry people between the islands and Piraeus, a port city south of Athens. Athens is the capital and largest city of Greece.

Greek Civilization

The world owes a lot to Greece. A long time ago, this small country was the center of civilization. During that time, the Greeks achieved many things that make a difference in our lives today. They developed drama, democracy, and architecture, which is a plan for how buildings are built.

Some of the Greeks' achievements can still be seen today. This hill in Athens with ancient buildings is called the Acropolis. One of these buildings, the Parthenon, is very famous. It is a temple that was built more than 2,000 years ago for the goddess Athena.

Athens, the capital of Greece, is always bustling with activity. After all, there are a lot of people here. Athens and the area around it are home to one-third of Greece's people. They ride modern cars and buses through streets lined with ancient buildings.

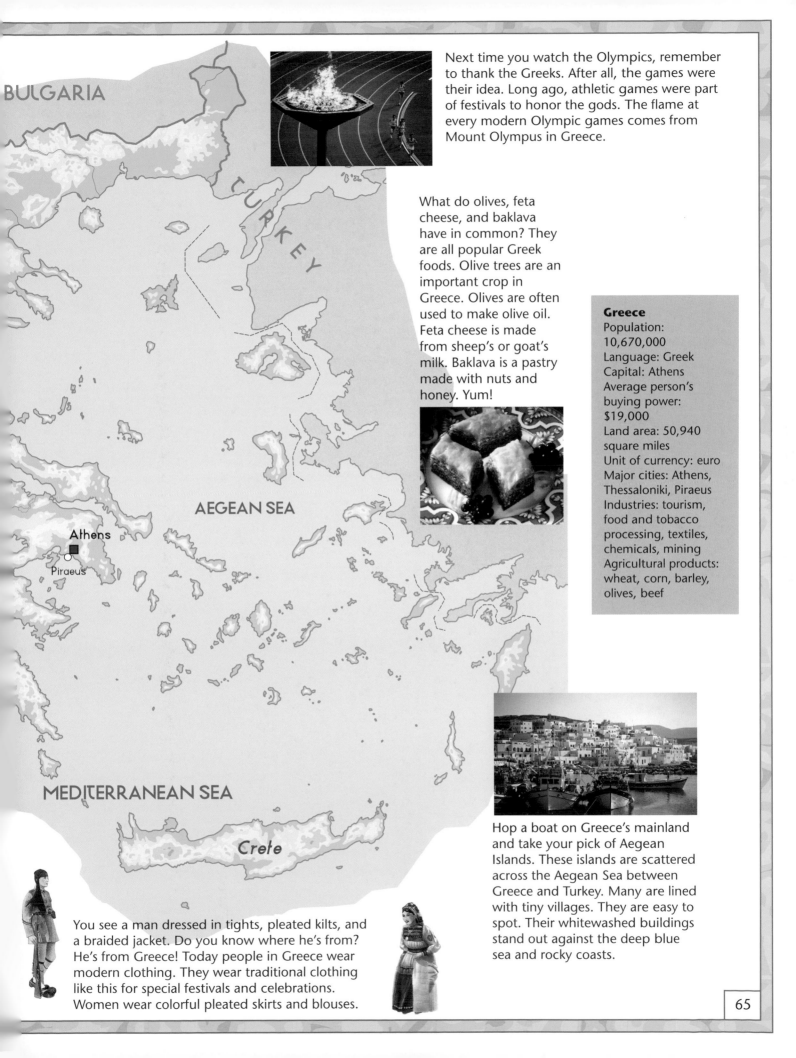

BULGARIA

TURKEY

Next time you watch the Olympics, remember to thank the Greeks. After all, the games were their idea. Long ago, athletic games were part of festivals to honor the gods. The flame at every modern Olympic games comes from Mount Olympus in Greece.

What do olives, feta cheese, and baklava have in common? They are all popular Greek foods. Olive trees are an important crop in Greece. Olives are often used to make olive oil. Feta cheese is made from sheep's or goat's milk. Baklava is a pastry made with nuts and honey. Yum!

Greece
Population: 10,670,000
Language: Greek
Capital: Athens
Average person's buying power: $19,000
Land area: 50,940 square miles
Unit of currency: euro
Major cities: Athens, Thessaloniki, Piraeus
Industries: tourism, food and tobacco processing, textiles, chemicals, mining
Agricultural products: wheat, corn, barley, olives, beef

AEGEAN SEA

Athens
Piraeus

MEDITERRANEAN SEA

Crete

Hop a boat on Greece's mainland and take your pick of Aegean Islands. These islands are scattered across the Aegean Sea between Greece and Turkey. Many are lined with tiny villages. They are easy to spot. Their whitewashed buildings stand out against the deep blue sea and rocky coasts.

You see a man dressed in tights, pleated kilts, and a braided jacket. Do you know where he's from? He's from Greece! Today people in Greece wear modern clothing. They wear traditional clothing like this for special festivals and celebrations. Women wear colorful pleated skirts and blouses.

Eastern Europe

The map of this part of Europe looks a lot different today than it did just a few years ago. Many of these countries used to be part of other countries, but today they are independent nations.

Bosnia and Herzegovina and Macedonia were part of Yugoslavia. Yugoslavia is now called Serbia and Montenegro. Belarus, Ukraine, and Moldova were all part of the former Soviet Union, a large communist country. Under communism people in a country do not get to say how the government is run. Albania, Bulgaria, and Romania were also communist countries until the early 1990s.

If you visit Bulgaria or Romania, bring your hiking shoes. These countries have a lot of mountains. The Carpathian Mountains form a crescent shape across Ukraine and into Romania. Many villages are nestled in their valleys. The Balkan Mountains stretch from the eastern border of Serbia and Montenegro across Bulgaria.

Eastern Orthodox Christians in Ukraine have the same beliefs as Eastern Orthodox Christians in Bulgaria. However, the two groups practice their faith in different ways. The name of their church usually includes their country's name, such as the Ukrainian Orthodox Church.

Look at this skyline. Do you see a pointed tower? It is called a minaret. Minarets are part of Islamic mosques. Many people in Bosnia and Albania are Muslims. They follow the religion of Islam. The mosque is their place of worship. Most mosques have from one to six minarets.

What's the main ingredient in bread? Wheat! So can you guess why Ukraine is known as the breadbasket of Europe? Because farmers here grow a lot of wheat! They also grow other grains, such as barley, corn, oats, rye, millet, and buckwheat.

Albania
Population: 3,590,000
Language: Albanian (some Greek)
Capital: Tirana
Average person's buying power: $4,500

Belarus
Population: 10,330,000
Language: Belarusian (some Russian)
Capital: Minsk
Average person's buying power: $8,200

Bosnia and Herzegovina
Population: 4,000,000
Language: Serbo-Croatian
Capital: Sarajevo
Average person's buying power: $1,900

Bulgaria
Population: 7,540,000
Language: Bulgarian
Capital: Sofia
Average person's buying power: $6,600

Macedonia
Population: 2,070,000
Language: Macedonian (some Albanian)
Capital: Skopje
Average person's buying power: $5,000

Moldova
Population: 4,440,000
Language: Moldovan (some Russian)
Capital: Chisinau
Average person's buying power: $2,500

Romania
Population: 22,280,000
Language: Romanian (some Hungarian)
Capital: Bucharest
Average person's buying power: $7,400

Serbia and Montenegro
Population: 10,660,000
Language: Serbian (some Albanian)
Capital: Belgrade
Average person's buying power: $2,370

Ukraine
Population: 48,060,000
Language: Ukrainian (some Russian)
Capital: Kiev
Average person's buying power: $4,500

In the Summer Olympics you can bet the Romanian gymnasts will tumble and flip their way to Olympic medals. The country is famous for its amazing athletes. Nadia Comaneci was a Romanian gymnast. In 1976, she became the first gymnast to earn a perfect score of 10 in the Olympic Games.

Folk Dancing

You see people dressed in colorful costumes. Suddenly the music starts. They squat down and kick out their feet. Then they jump into the air. They are performing a Ukrainian folk dance. Folk dancing and music are important here. They helped each Eastern European country keep its culture alive while the Soviet Union ruled this part of the world.

Russian Federation

The Russian Federation, or Russia, is the largest country in the world. It is almost twice as big as Canada. Russia is so big, it stretches across two continents, Europe and Asia. Two-thirds of Russia's territory is in Asia. If you traveled all the way across Russia, you would have to adjust your watch 11 times! This is because Russia has 11 different time zones.

The Ural Mountains divide Russia into two regions. West of these mountains is European Russia. This is where most Russians live. The rest live to the east of the mountains, in Asia. This area is a vast wilderness known as Siberia.

Ballet is a dance of skill and beauty. No other country produces ballet dancers quite the way Russia does. Russian ballet troupes, such as the Bolshoi Ballet, are world famous. These dancers are part of the famous Kirov Ballet.

Eggs are fun to color. But in Russia, they are works of art! Russian jeweler Peter Carl Faberge decorated some of the most famous eggs with Russian gold and jewels over 100 years ago.

The Kremlin and Red Square

The Kremlin and Red Square are must-sees in Moscow. The Kremlin is a huge walled fortress

that stands at the heart of the city. Inside it are palaces, churches and cathedrals, and hundreds of years of Russian history. Today it is the center of the Russian government. Red Square is a very large plaza right next to it. This is a large, open space where people can gather. It is where the Soviet Union used to have parades to show off its military power. St. Basil's Cathedral stands at one end of Red Square, right next to the Kremlin.

BALTIC SEA
FINLAND
ESTONIA
Kaliningrad
LITHUANIA
LATVIA
St. Petersburg
BELARUS
Moscow ■
BARENTS SEA
Nizhny Novgorod
Volga
UKRAINE
SEA OF AZOV
Ural Mountains
Yekaterinbu
Chelyabinsk
BLACK SEA
Caucasus
GEORGIA
TURKEY
ARMENIA
AZERBAIJAN
CASPIAN SEA
IRAN
KAZAKHSTA

0   120   240   360 miles

They look like big onions in the sky. What are they? They are domes that are unique to Russian Orthodox architecture. They represent the flame of a burning candle. Domes like these are a sure sign that you are looking at a Russian Orthodox church. These colorful onion-shape domes are on St. Basil's Cathedral in Moscow.

ДА
НЕТ
МАЛЬЧИК
ДЕВОЧКА

If you want to read Russian, you will have to learn a new alphabet! The Russian alphabet has 33 letters.

This is how you write the Russian words for *yes, no, boy,* and *girl.*

You have to enjoy the cold to live in Siberia. The temperature here can drop to –90°F! But believe it or not, people do live here. They include native peoples such as Buryats, Yakuts, and Nentsi. Many of them make their living by herding reindeer or catching fish.

Population: 144,530,000
Language: Russian (many other languages spoken by small groups of people)
Capital: Moscow
Average person's buying power: $9,300
Land area: 6,592,800 square miles
Unit of currency: Russian ruble

Major cities: Moscow, St. Petersburg, Nizhny Novgorod, Novosibirsk, Yekaterinburg
Industries: mining, heavy machinery, shipbuilding, transportation equipment, communications equipment
Agricultural products: grain, sugar beets, beef, sunflower seed, vegetables

ARCTIC OCEAN

EAST SIBERIAN SEA

BERING SEA

LAPTEV SEA

KARA SEA

SEA OF OKHOTSK

RUSSIAN FEDERATION

Siberia

Lena
Lena
Lena
Lena
Ob
Ob

Novosibirsk

Lake Baikal

CHINA

JAPAN
JAPAN SEA

Vladivostok

MONGOLIA

NORTH KOREA

CHINA

Look at this colorful wooden doll. Open her up, and there's another doll, and another, and another. This traditional Russian doll is called a matreshka. These dolls can have as many as 12 or more dolls nesting inside one another!

It is not easy to forget that Russia was once a communist country. There are many reminders. Lenin was a communist leader. His tomb, or grave, sits in Red Square. A hammer and sickle, which is a tool with a curved blade, was a symbol of Russian communism.

Asia

Asia's name is small, but it is the largest continent! It reaches almost halfway around the globe, covering nearly one-third of the planet's land. It stretches from Africa and Europe in the west to the Pacific Ocean in the east. From north to south, it stretches from the Arctic Ocean to the Indian Ocean.

If you visited Asia, you would find all kinds of climates, from steamy tropical beaches in Vietnam to freezing-cold tundra in Siberia. You could climb to the highest point in the world, Mount Everest, and visit the lowest, the Dead Sea. You could also swim in the world's largest lake, the Caspian Sea.

Human civilization began in Asia, about 7,500 years ago. Asia was the birthplace of many important ancient peoples. Most of the world's major religions, including Hinduism, Buddhism, Judaism, Christianity, and Islam, were first practiced on this continent.

Some countries in Asia, such as Japan, South Korea, Taiwan, and Singapore, are highly developed industrialized nations and produce everything from cars to electronics. The countries of the Middle East produce much of the world's oil.

Today, Asia is home to more than half of the earth's people. Asians are as varied as everything else about the continent.

ARCTIC OCEAN

RUSSIAN
FEDERATION

MONGOLIA

CHINA

NORTH KOREA

SOUTH
KOREA

JAPAN

PACIFIC
OCEAN

NEPAL

BHUTAN

BANGLADESH

MYANMAR
(BURMA)

LAOS

VIETNAM

THAILAND

CAMBODIA

SOUTH
CHINA
SEA

TAIWAN

PHILIPPINES

SRI LANKA

MALAYSIA

BRUNEI

SINGAPORE

INDONESIA

PAPUA NEW GUINEA

INDIAN
OCEAN

JAVA SEA

BANDA SEA

EAST
TIMOR

ARAFURA SEA

TIMOR
SEA

AUSTRALIA

Highest point: Mount Everest, 29,035 feet

Lowest point: Dead Sea, 1,339 feet below sea level

Major rivers: Chang, or Yangtze (China), 3,720 miles; Yenisei-Angara (Russia), 3,650 miles; Amur-Argun (Russia, China), 3,590 miles; Ob-Irtysh (Russia, Kazakhstan, China), 3,360 miles

Biggest lakes: Caspian Sea (Kazakhstan, Turkmenistan, Iran, Azerbaijan, Russia), 143,240 square miles; Aral Sea (Uzbekistan, Kazakhstan), 24,904 square miles; Lake Baikal (Russia), 12,160 square miles

Major mountains: Mount Everest (China, Nepal), 29,035 feet; K2 (China, Pakistan), 28,250 feet; Kanchenjunga (India, Nepal), 28,208 feet

Total land area: 17,212,040 square miles

Total population: 3,841,000,000

Largest country (area): Russia, 6,592,800 square miles (Russia is in Asia and Europe; area of Asian Russia is about 5,000,000 square miles)

Smallest country (area): Maldives, 116 square miles

Largest country (population): China, 1,286,980,000

Smallest country (population): Maldives, 330,000

0   250   500   750   1000 miles

Japan, North Korea, and South Korea

Japan does not have a lot of land. But it sure has a lot of people! Japan is a chain of islands that sits just off the coast of mainland Asia. There are four main islands and 4,000 smaller ones. Towering volcanoes make the islands of Japan absolutely beautiful. However, they also make it a land of violent natural forces. Japan experiences frequent earthquakes, volcanoes, and fierce storms called typhoons.

Korea is a peninsula that stretches from China toward Japan. It also has more than 3,000 islands. The land is divided between two separate countries: North Korea and South Korea.

Origami

Take a piece of paper. Fold it this way and that way. Now what do you have? It's origami, the Japanese art of folding paper into objects. The word *origami* means "folded paper" in Japanese. With origami you can turn a square piece of paper into almost anything—a cup, a ship, a bird, or a flower! In fact there are about 100 traditional origami figures. Origami actually started in China, but it really took off in Japan. Find a book on origami in your library and try this Japanese art form yourself!

CHINA

Chongjin

NORTH KOREA

Hamhung

Pyongyang

SEA OF JAPAN

Inchon Seoul

SOUTH KOREA

Pusan

EAST CHINA SEA

Nagasaki

Kyushu

0 15 30 45 miles

Imagine flying on a bullet. That's almost what it is like to ride the bullet train in Japan. This country is a leader in developing high-speed trains. The bullet train, called *shinkansen* in Japanese, can reach 186 miles per hour!

The instruments below may look a little bit like guitars, but they are kotos, used to play traditional Japanese music. This large Japanese instrument has 13 strings. To play it, you pluck the strings with the fingers of both hands.

RUSSIA

SEA OF OKHOTSK

Sapporo

Hokkaido

PACIFIC OCEAN

H o n s h u

J A P A N

Tokyo

Nagoya

Mt. Fuji

Yokohama

Osaka

Shikoku

Japanese people wear traditional clothes for holidays and special events. Women wear kimonos, long robes with wide sleeves. They are worn with an obi, or sash. Boys sometimes carry a curved samurai sword. Samurai were Japanese warriors. Young women, called geishas, painted their faces white.

If you are in Tokyo and want to shop, go to the Ginza district. There are a lot of stores here. You will see many bright lights here, too. The Ginza is one of Tokyo's liveliest and most colorful districts. It is also famous for its restaurants and nightlife.

Japan
Population: 127,220,000
Language: Japanese
Capital: Tokyo
Average person's buying power: $28,000
Land area: 145,880 square miles
Unit of currency: yen
Major cities: Tokyo, Yokohama, Osaka, Nagoya, Sapporo
Industries: motor vehicles, electronic equipment, machine tools, steel and nonferrous metals, textiles
Agricultural products: rice, sugar beets, pork, poultry, fish

North Korea
Population: 22,470,000
Language: Korean
Capital: Pyongyang
Average person's buying power: $1,000
Land Area: 46,540 square miles
Unit of currency: North Korean won
Major cities: Pyongyang, Hamhung, Chongjin

South Korea
Population: 48,290,000
Language: Korean
Capital: Seoul
Average person's buying power: $19,400
Land area: 38,030 square miles
Unit of currency: South Korean won
Major cities: Seoul, Pusan, Inchon

Are you ready to climb? Mount Fuji is the highest mountain in Japan. The Japanese people see it as a symbol of the beauty of their land. They think that everyone should climb it at least once. Do you think you'll ever make the climb?

Karaoke, sushi, karate…these are all from Japan. However, they have become such a part of American culture, it might be hard to remember that. In karaoke, a person sings with recorded music. Sushi is a dish of rice and raw fish or vegetables. Karate is a form of martial arts.

Southeast Asia

The five countries of mainland Southeast Asia cover part of a peninsula that sticks out into the South China Sea. Three of these countries, Laos, Cambodia, and Vietnam, were sometimes grouped together and called "Indochina."

Most people in Southeast Asia live in the river valleys or along the coasts. They make their homes in small villages and work on farms. The most important food crop is rice. But there are some big cities here, too. They include Bangkok in Thailand, Phnom Penh in Cambodia, and Ho Chi Minh City and Hanoi in Vietnam.

Laos is a tropical land of mountains and forests. Heavy rains often fall here. Almost all the people are farmers. They grow rice along the Mekong River. Laotians live in houses that sit on wooden posts six to eight feet above the ground to protect them from floods.

Everyone loves a puppet show! This is especially true in southern Thailand. But the puppet shows they enjoy here are not like western puppet shows. The puppets are hidden behind a white screen and lit up from behind, as shown here. Therefore, the audience sees only the puppets' shadows.

Myanmar (Burma)
Population: 42,520,000
Language: Burmese (some local languages)
Capital: Rangoon
Average person's buying power: $1,660

Cambodia
Population: 13,130,000
Language: Khmer (some French)
Capital: Phnom Penh
Average person's buying power: $1,500

Laos
Population: 5,930,000
Language: Lao (some French)
Capital: Vientiane
Average person's buying power: $1,700

Thailand
Population: 64,270,000
Language: Thai
Capital: Bangkok
Average person's buying power: $6,900

Vietnam
Population: 81,630,000
Language: Vietnamese
Capital: Hanoi
Average person's buying power: $2,250

CHINA

INDIA

BANGLADESH

Mandalay

MYANMAR
(BURMA)

VIETNAM

LAOS

THAILAND

CAMBODIA

MALAYSIA

Gulf of Tonkin

SOUTH CHINA SEA

Bay
of
Bengal

ANDAMAN
SEA

Gulf
of
Thailand

0 40 80 120 miles

Rangoon

Chiang Mai

Vientiane

Bangkok

Chao Phraya

Mekong

Mekong

Mekong

Angkor

Phnom Penh

Ho Chi Minh City

Hue

Annamite Cordillera

Phuket
Island

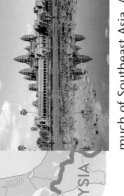

The Buddhist temples of Thailand are beautiful and extraordinary! Almost everyone in Thailand follows the religion of Buddhism. Temples usually feature statues of Buddha. Here is a golden Buddha.

Khmer kings built the city of Angkor in the ninth century when they controlled much of Southeast Asia. Angkor's most magnificent temple was Angkor Wat. In 1431, Angkor was invaded and captured. But the invaders soon abandoned it. The jungle gradually grew over the city and the temples, hiding it for centuries.

For special occasions, many Thai people wear traditional dress. This may include garments made from colorful silk with gold embroidery. Thai dancers wear very elaborate costumes. Dancing is an important part of holidays and special celebrations.

Imagine buying groceries from a floating store. You could if you lived in Bangkok, Thailand. At one time the city had many canals around the mouth of the Chao Phraya River. The canals were marketplaces where people with small boats could sell produce.

Rice Farming

You can see them working in the fields. Their straw hats seem to dance under the hot, hot sun. Who are they? They are the men and women who work the rice fields of Southeast Asia.

Rice is Asia's most important food crop. Growing rice is hot, hard work. It needs lots of water and sunshine. The rice fields of Southeast Asia are called paddies. The rice farmer plants rice seeds in a seedbed. After they have started to grow, the plants are moved to a rice paddy to finish growing.

77

Malaysia, Singapore, and Brunei

A strait is a channel of water that connects two bodies of water. The Strait of Malacca runs between Malaysia and the island of Sumatra. It connects the South China Sea and the Indian Ocean. As these ships show, it is an important shipping route.

Port of Singapore

Location, location, location. This is what some people say is the key to success. It is indeed true for Singapore. Located where the South China Sea and the Indian Ocean meet, Singapore is one of the world's busiest ports. More than 300 million tons of cargo pass through this harbor in a single year. That's a lot of VCRs, clothes, and computers.

At the busiest times, ships form lines all the way out to sea. They wait to unload cargo, make repairs, or pick up new cargo. The cargo they carry includes such products as chemicals, foods, furniture, shoes, machinery, cars, and steel.

If you like your weather hot and sticky, this part of the world is for you! Malaysia and Singapore lie near the equator. These countries, like others near the equator, have warm, wet weather all year.

THAILAND

Malay Peninsula

MALAYSIA

SOUTH CHINA

SEA

Kuala Lumpur

Sumatra

Strait of Malacca

Singapore

SINGAPORE

I N

0   36   72   108 mi

The Petronas Towers are in Kuala Lumpur, the capital of Malaysia. Completed in 1996, the two connected buildings stand 1,482 feet high. They were the tallest in the world until Taipei 101 opened in Taiwan on December 31, 2004.

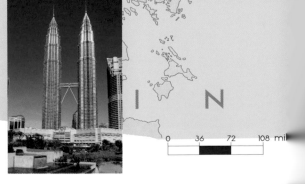

Malaysia is one country, but it is made up of two regions that are between 400 and 600 miles apart. The South China Sea stands between them. One region is called Peninsular Malaysia or West Malaysia. It sits on the southern part of the Malay Peninsula. The other is called Sarawak and Sabah or East Malaysia. It is on the northern part of the island of Borneo. It shares the island with other countries.

The island nation of Singapore is made up of one large island and more than 50 smaller islands. Most of its people are Chinese.

Brunei lies on the north coast of the island of Borneo, surrounded by Malaysia.

Brunei may be very small, but there is a lot of oil underground. This natural resource has made some people here very wealthy. Soon, the oil in Brunei will run out. The government is trying to develop new industries before this happens.

What if your house had to sit in water all the time? It would get pretty wet. Stilts are long posts used to support a building above wet land. Parts of Malaysia are covered in swampland. Many houses in rural areas of Malaysia are built on stilts.

The Penan live in the rain forests on the island of Borneo. The entire rain forest is their home, because they do not stay in one place. Everything they need is in the forest. There are not many Penan left. The rain forests are being destroyed for their lumber.

Brunei
Population: 360,000
Languages: Malay, Chinese
Capital: Bandar Seri Begawan
Average person's buying power: $18,600

Malaysia
Population: 23,100,000
Language: Bahasa Malayu
Capital: Kuala Lumpur
Average person's buying power: $9,300

Singapore
Population: 4,610,000
Languages: Chinese, Malay, Tamil, English
Capital: Singapore
Average person's buying power: $24,000

SULU SEA

PHILIPPINES

BRUNEI
Bandar Seri Begawan

SABAH

SARAWAK

MALAYSIA

B o r n e o

O N E S I A

Philippines

The Philippines is made up of more than 7,000 islands. Most of them are just tiny dots on a map. If you wanted to see a list of all the islands of the Philippines, you would not be able to find one. Just a little more than half the islands have names. Only about 1,000 of them even have any people living there.

The people of the Philippines are called Filipinos. Many live in rural areas and farm for a living. However, a lot of Filipinos prefer the activity of the city.

Ring of Fire

Living in the Ring of Fire sounds pretty scary, doesn't it? Well, the countries that lie within this area of the world are not exactly surrounded by fire. But there are a lot of volcanoes and earthquakes. And that can be scary indeed.

The Ring of Fire is the name of a chain of volcanoes that encircles the Pacific Ocean. Islands in the Philippines are part of this chain. The earth's crust is divided into huge sections of rock, called plates. When the plates move, they make volcanoes form around their edges or cause earthquakes. The Ring of Fire is at the edge of some of these plates.

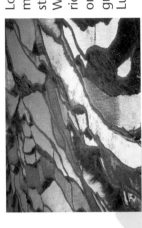

Look at the giant steps up the mountainside. They aren't really steps. They are terraced rice paddies. With so many mountains, Filipino rice farmers have to grow their crops on slopes of land. Rice has been grown like this on the island of Luzon for more than 2,000 years!

You might think the water here would not be deep. After all, there are so many islands. But just east of the islands lies some of the deepest water in the Pacific Ocean. The Philippine trench is more than 34,000 feet deep. Many odd fish, such as this anglerfish, can live at these depths.

PHILIPPINE

Luzon

Quezon City
Manila

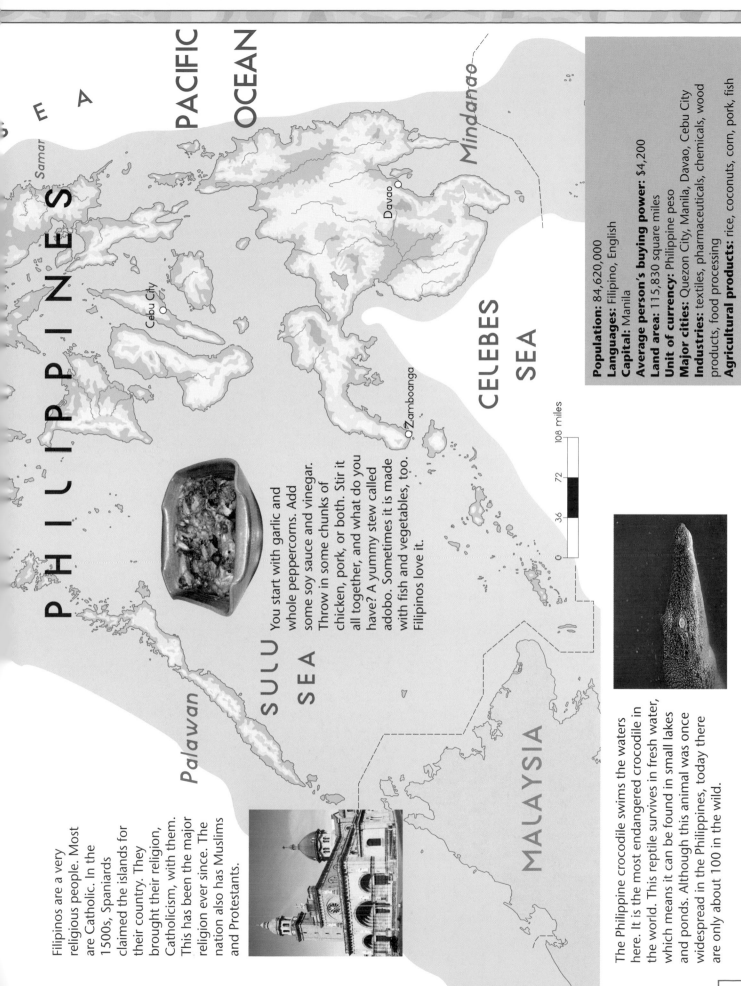

PHILIPPINES

PACIFIC OCEAN

Samar

Cebu City

Davao

Mindanao

Zamboanga

CELEBES SEA

SULU SEA

Palawan

MALAYSIA

0 36 72 108 miles

Filipinos are a very religious people. Most are Catholic. In the 1500s, Spaniards claimed the islands for their country. They brought their religion, Catholicism, with them. This has been the major religion ever since. The nation also has Muslims and Protestants.

You start with garlic and whole peppercorns. Add some soy sauce and vinegar. Throw in some chunks of chicken, pork, or both. Stir it all together, and what do you have? A yummy stew called adobo. Sometimes it is made with fish and vegetables, too. Filipinos love it.

The Philippine crocodile swims the waters here. It is the most endangered crocodile in the world. This reptile survives in fresh water, which means it can be found in small lakes and ponds. Although this animal was once widespread in the Philippines, today there are only about 100 in the wild.

Population: 84,620,000
Languages: Filipino, English
Capital: Manila
Average person's buying power: $4,200
Land area: 115,830 square miles
Unit of currency: Philippine peso
Major cities: Quezon City, Manila, Davao, Cebu City
Industries: textiles, pharmaceuticals, chemicals, wood products, food processing
Agricultural products: rice, coconuts, corn, pork, fish

Indonesia

Like many countries in Asia, Indonesia is an archipelago. An archipelago is a group of many islands. Indonesia is the world's largest group, made up of more than 17,500 islands. They lie along the equator between the Indian and Pacific oceans. They stretch for more than 3,000 miles to form a bridge between the continents of Australia and Asia.

Indonesia has one of the largest populations in the world. People live on more than 6,000 of its islands. Most live on the island of Java, one of Indonesia's largest islands. East Timor recently gained its independence from Indonesia.

THAILAND

SOUTH CHINA SEA

MALAYSIA

Medan

SINGAPORE

Bo

I N D O C

Sumatra Palembang

INDIAN OCEAN

JAVA SEA

Jakarta

Bandung Semarang

Surabaya

Java

Java and Jakarta

Java has the largest population of the Indonesian islands. The Javanese make up the largest ethnic group. But they are not the only ethnic group in Indonesia. Few countries have such a variety of cultures. That's why Indonesia's motto is "Unity in Diversity."

Jakarta, the country's capital and business center, is located on Java. Indonesia's largest city is a mix of old and new. Tall, modern buildings tower over older, traditional homes.

Indonesia is the world's largest Islamic nation. People who practice Islam worship in mosques. The early mosques of Indonesia were made of wood. Today few of these still stand. They have been replaced by brick or stone buildings, which are more like the mosques of the Middle East.

Thousands of villages cover the island of Java. It is by far Indonesia's most industrialized island. Across the water lies Borneo. Life here is quite different from Java. Tropical rain forests and mountains cover a lot of the land. And many fewer people call this island home.

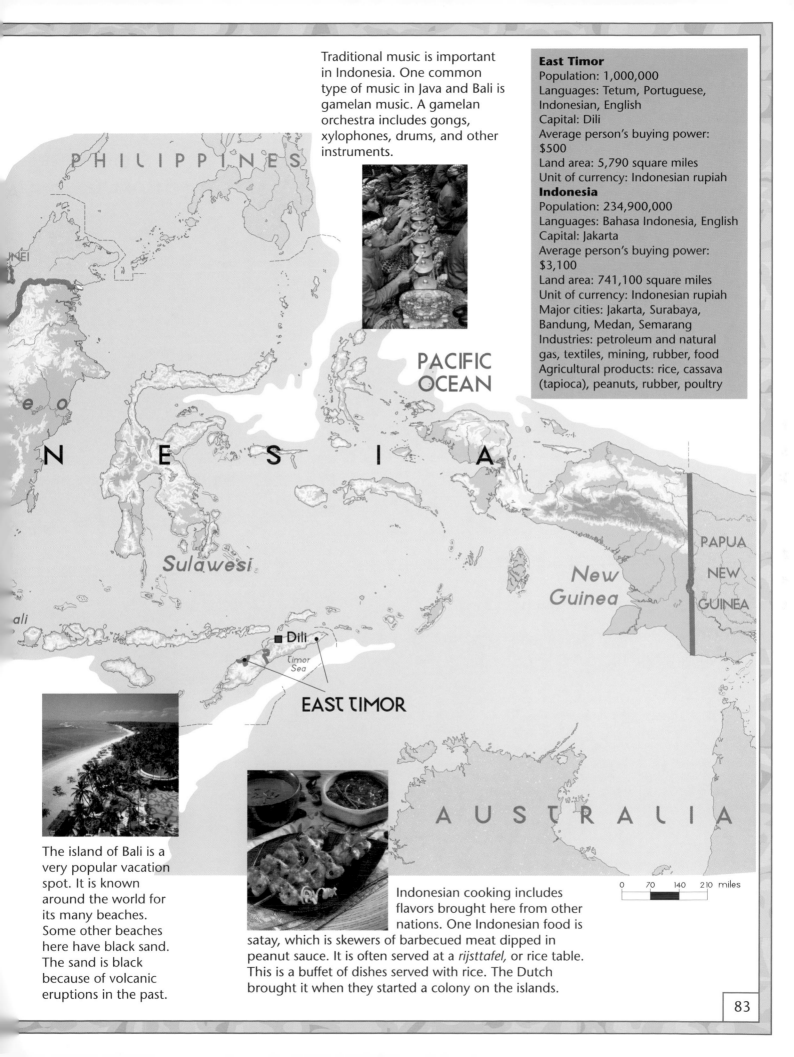

Traditional music is important in Indonesia. One common type of music in Java and Bali is gamelan music. A gamelan orchestra includes gongs, xylophones, drums, and other instruments.

East Timor
Population: 1,000,000
Languages: Tetum, Portuguese, Indonesian, English
Capital: Dili
Average person's buying power: $500
Land area: 5,790 square miles
Unit of currency: Indonesian rupiah

Indonesia
Population: 234,900,000
Languages: Bahasa Indonesia, English
Capital: Jakarta
Average person's buying power: $3,100
Land area: 741,100 square miles
Unit of currency: Indonesian rupiah
Major cities: Jakarta, Surabaya, Bandung, Medan, Semarang
Industries: petroleum and natural gas, textiles, mining, rubber, food
Agricultural products: rice, cassava (tapioca), peanuts, rubber, poultry

PHILIPPINES

PACIFIC OCEAN

NESIA

Sulawesi

New Guinea

PAPUA NEW GUINEA

Dili
Timor Sea
EAST TIMOR

AUSTRALIA

0   70   140   210 miles

The island of Bali is a very popular vacation spot. It is known around the world for its many beaches. Some other beaches here have black sand. The sand is black because of volcanic eruptions in the past.

Indonesian cooking includes flavors brought here from other nations. One Indonesian food is satay, which is skewers of barbecued meat dipped in peanut sauce. It is often served at a *rijsttafel,* or rice table. This is a buffet of dishes served with rice. The Dutch brought it when they started a colony on the islands.

Northern India, Bangladesh, Nepal, and Bhutan

India is a large country with a large population. With more than one billion people, India has a wide variety of people and cultures. India has 15 official languages, as well as English, which is widely spoken. On India's northern border lie three small countries: Bangladesh, Bhutan, and Nepal.

The Himalayan Mountains stretch across Bhutan and Nepal. This is the world's highest mountain range. Bangladesh is a poor country with one of the world's largest populations. It is often hit by natural disasters. The people here have seen many cyclones and floods. Kashmir is a region that stands between Pakistan and India. The two countries have been fighting for control of this land for years.

Sikhism is one of the religions of India. The Golden Temple in the city of Amritsar is the holiest Sikh shrine. Sikh men do not cut their hair. They wear a turban on their heads.

Taj Mahal

This beautiful structure is the Taj Mahal. And the love story behind it is just as beautiful.

The Taj Mahal stands in Agra, in northern India. Shah Jahan was emperor of this part of India from 1627 to 1658. His wife and queen was Mumtaz Mahal. The two were very much in love. But Mumtaz died while giving birth to their 14th child. As she was dying, she asked Jahan to build a lasting tomb in memory of their love.

Jahan ordered workers to carry out her wish. About 20,000 workers built the Taj Mahal over more than 20 years. Today both Jahan and Mumtaz are buried there.

NORTHERN AREAS
Occupied by Pakistan and claimed by India

Kashmi

JAMMU AND KASHMIR
Occupied by India and claimed by Pakistan

PAKISTAN

Amritsar

Great Indian Desert

New Delhi
Delhi

Pushkar

Jaipur

Ahmadabad

Bh

ARABIAN SEA

Mumbai (Bombay)

India
Population: 1,049,710,000
Languages: Hindi, English, Bengali, Telugu, Marathi, Tamil, Urdu, Gujarati, Malayalam, Kannada, Oriya, Punjabi, Assamese, Kashmiri, Sindhi, Sanskrit
Capital: New Delhi
Average person's buying power: $2,540
Land area: 1,269,350 square miles
Unit of currency: Indian rupee
Major cities: Mumbai (Bombay), Delhi, Kolkata (Calcutta), Chennai (Madras), Bangalore
Industries: textiles, chemicals, food processing, steel, transportation equipment
Agricultural products: rice, wheat, oilseed, cattle, fish

Bangladesh
Population: 138,450,000
Languages: Bangla, English
Capital: Dhaka
Average person's buying power: $1,700
Land area: 55,600 square miles
Unit of currency: taka
Major cities: Dhaka, Chittagong, Khulna
Industries: cotton textiles, jute, garments, tea processing, paper newsprint
Agricultural products: rice, jute, tea, wheat, beef

Bhutan
Population: 2,140,000
Language: Dzongkha
Capital: Thimphu
Average person's buying power: $1,300

Nepal
Population: 26,470,000
Language: Nepali
Capital: Kathmandu
Average person's buying power: $1,400

Would you walk for miles to bathe in a river? If you practiced the religion of Hinduism you might. Nearly 80 percent of people in India, almost 800 million, are Hindu. They journey from all parts of India to the holy city of Varanasi. They come here to bathe in the Ganges River, where they believe the water is sacred.

You can do some incredible mountain climbing in Nepal. After all, the world's highest mountain—Mount Everest—lies between Nepal and Tibet. It is part of the Himalayas. The top of Mount Everest is 29,035 feet above sea level. It is the highest point in the world.

Indian cities are home to a lot of people. The streets can often become crowded as the people move from one place to another. People can take trolleys, taxicabs, cars, or trucks to get where they need to go. Many people simply decide to walk.

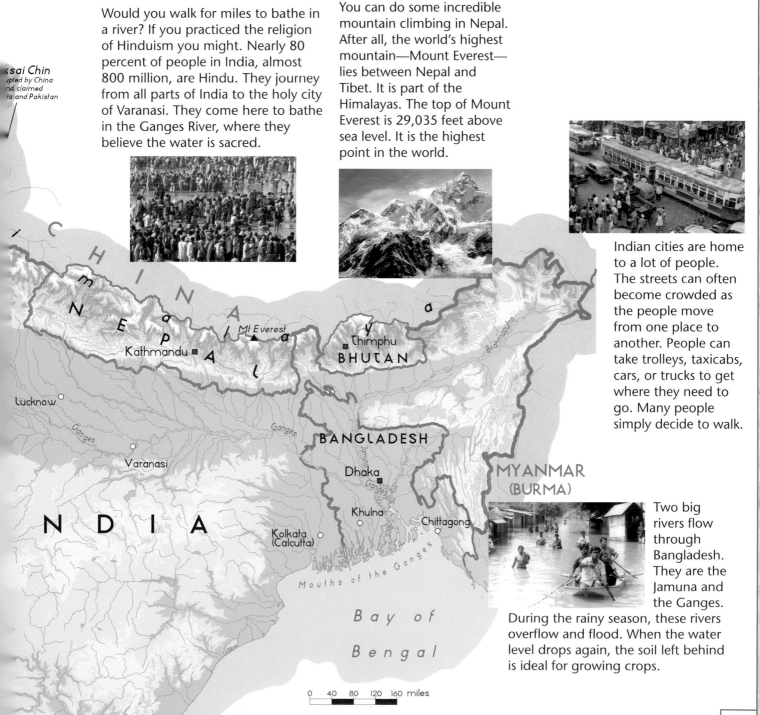

Two big rivers flow through Bangladesh. They are the Jamuna and the Ganges. During the rainy season, these rivers overflow and flood. When the water level drops again, the soil left behind is ideal for growing crops.

Southern India

Many of the world's movies each year are made in Mumbai. Sometimes people call the city Bollywood. That is a combination of Mumbai's old name—Bombay—and Hollywood. Moviemakers in India produce hundreds of films in many languages. The most popular movies are those in the Hindi language.

India is a land of great variety. A vast, barren desert lies in the west. But parts of eastern India get some of the highest rainfall in the world.

India is the seventh-largest country in the world. It ranks second in population. Because India is so big, it is divided into different land areas. The area in the southern part of the country is called the Deccan Plateau. A plateau is a flat area of land that is higher than the land around it. Just off the southeast coast of southern India is the island country of Sri Lanka. Southeast is the tiny country of Maldives.

Mumbai (Bombay)

INDIA

○ Hyderabad

ARABIAN SEA

Western Ghats

Eastern Ghats

0 40 80 120 160 miles

Bangalore

Chennai (Madras)

Calicut

Trivandrum

SRI LANKA

MALDIVES

Male

Colombo
Sri Jayewardenepura Kott

Everything about Maldives is small. It is the smallest country in Asia, and one of the smallest in the world. It is made up of 1,200 small islands grouped together in clusters called atolls. The highest point on these islands is less than eight feet above the sea.

Some of the hardest workers in India are elephants. These gentle giants can travel to hilly areas that motor vehicles cannot reach. Foresters may use elephants to move logs and carry heavy loads. They were also once used to carry hunters through the forest and soldiers into battle.

MYANMAR (BURMA)

Indian music uses instruments you may not have heard before, such as the sitar, shown here. This is a stringed instrument that is plucked. The tabla and the mridangam are drums. Indian dances are often based on Hindu stories.

B a y

o f

B e n g a l

ANDAMAN SEA

Andaman Islands (India)

Sri Lanka is sometimes called the "pearl of the Indian Ocean." And in fact, many gems are found here. Sri Lanka is home to 40 types of gems, such as rubies and diamonds. Many Sri Lankans work in the jewelry business. However, most people here are farmers. Tea is an important crop for them.

Cloth made in India is fit for a king! Long ago, the emperors of Rome and China wore Indian clothing. Textiles made here include cotton, silk, and wool. They are woven, hand painted, or embroidered in brilliant colors and fancy designs. One such cloth is called brocade. It has raised designs woven into it.

Bengal Tigers

Bengal tigers prowl the jungles of India. Tigers live only in Asia. They are not native to Africa. Bengal tigers live mostly in India, but other kinds live throughout Asia.

When people think of a tiger, they often picture the Bengal tiger. These animals have bright reddish-orange fur with dark black stripes. Not including the tail, males can grow to about six-and-a-half feet long. With tails extended, they can be almost ten feet long.

Bengal tigers are an endangered species. India has made some tiger reserves in national parks to protect them.

Afghanistan and Pakistan

Afghanistan and Pakistan lie next to each other in southern Asia. While Afghanistan is landlocked, Pakistan lies on the shores of the Arabian Sea.

Rugged mountains rise in central Afghanistan. North of the mountains, areas of grass and farmland grow. Sandy deserts cover the area south of the mountains. Afghanistan has had a difficult and violent history. Its troubles continue today.

Pakistan has been called the crossroads of Asia. This is because travelers over the centuries from India, China, and Europe have passed through this country in search of new land. Most Pakistanis live and farm the land in the Indus River Valley.

The different ethnic groups of Afghanistan do not always agree. But they have come up with a way to settle problems. It is called *loya jirga,* which means "grand council." This council is made up of leaders from the different groups. They come together to talk and share ideas.

Afghanistan
Population: 28,720,000
Languages: Afghan Persian (Dari), Pashtu, Tajik, Uzbek
Capital: Kabul
Average person's buying power: $700
Land area: 250,000 square miles
Unit of currency: afghani
Major cities: Kabul, Kandahar, Mazar-e Sharif
Industries: textiles, soap, furniture, hand-woven carpets, natural gas
Agricultural products: wheat, fruits, nuts, wool, mutton

Pakistan
Population: 150,700,000
Languages: Urdu, English, Punjabi, Sindhi, Pashtu
Capital: Islamabad
Average person's buying power: $2,100
Land area: 310,400 square miles
Unit of currency: Pakistani rupee
Major cities: Karachi, Lahore, Faisalabad, Rawalpindi
Industries: textiles and apparel, food processing, beverages, construction materials, paper products
Agricultural products: cotton, wheat, rice, milk, beef

ARABIAN SEA

0   35   70   105 miles

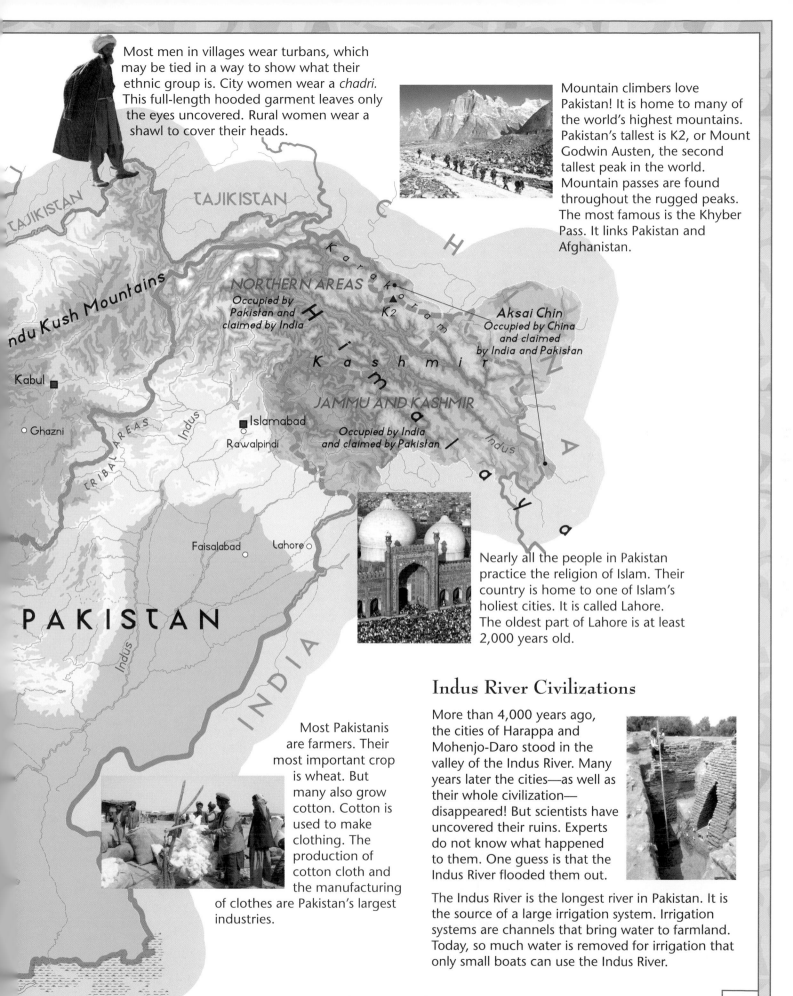

Most men in villages wear turbans, which may be tied in a way to show what their ethnic group is. City women wear a *chadri*. This full-length hooded garment leaves only the eyes uncovered. Rural women wear a shawl to cover their heads.

Mountain climbers love Pakistan! It is home to many of the world's highest mountains. Pakistan's tallest is K2, or Mount Godwin Austen, the second tallest peak in the world. Mountain passes are found throughout the rugged peaks. The most famous is the Khyber Pass. It links Pakistan and Afghanistan.

TAJIKISTAN

TAJIKISTAN

ndu Kush Mountains

Karakoram

NORTHERN AREAS
Occupied by
Pakistan and
claimed by India

K2

Aksai Chin
Occupied by China
and claimed
by India and Pakistan

Kabul

Ghazni

TRIBAL AREAS

Indus

Islamabad

Rawalpindi

JAMMU AND KASHMIR
Occupied by India
and claimed by Pakistan

Kashmir

Himalaya

Indus

Faisalabad

Lahore

PAKISTAN

Indus

INDIA

Nearly all the people in Pakistan practice the religion of Islam. Their country is home to one of Islam's holiest cities. It is called Lahore. The oldest part of Lahore is at least 2,000 years old.

Indus River Civilizations

Most Pakistanis are farmers. Their most important crop is wheat. But many also grow cotton. Cotton is used to make clothing. The production of cotton cloth and the manufacturing of clothes are Pakistan's largest industries.

More than 4,000 years ago, the cities of Harappa and Mohenjo-Daro stood in the valley of the Indus River. Many years later the cities—as well as their whole civilization— disappeared! But scientists have uncovered their ruins. Experts do not know what happened to them. One guess is that the Indus River flooded them out.

The Indus River is the longest river in Pakistan. It is the source of a large irrigation system. Irrigation systems are channels that bring water to farmland. Today, so much water is removed for irrigation that only small boats can use the Indus River.

Former Soviet Asia

A lot has changed in the countries of Central Asia over the past several years. For nearly 200 years, many countries here were under the control of the Russian Empire. In 1917, when Russia became the Soviet Union, they were part of it as well. The Soviet Union had a communist government. This means that the government controlled most things. The people did not get to choose who ran their government. In 1991 the Soviet Union broke apart. Russia and these eight nations became separate and independent.

Most people in former Soviet Asia are Muslims. They practice the religion of Islam. Some of the most beautiful Islamic mosques are found in Central Asia. Most are covered with dazzling mosaics of colorful tile.

The cities of former Soviet Asia are a mix of old and new. Samarkand and Tashkent in Uzbekistan have existed for thousands of years. Today, ancient gates and thousand-year-old mosques stand next to modern structures.

Horses are popular in this part of the world. All across the region, horseback riders gallop at high speed in a game that goes by many names. Played for centuries, this game is a lot like polo. Two teams of players hit a ball with a long racket.

Silk Road

What comes to mind when you hear the term *Silk Road*? Do you picture a road made of soft, shiny silk? Well, the Silk Road wasn't really made of silk. It was a major trade route for carrying silk, cotton, jade, glass, and other expensive goods. The Silk Road linked China with central Asia, the Middle East, and the Mediterranean Sea. Merchants traveled the road from the 300s to the 1400s. This is part of an old map that shows explorer Marco Polo and his brothers, who were later travelers on the Silk Road.

Astana

K H S T A N

Bishkek

KYRGYZSTAN

Tashkent

C H I N A

amarkand

TAJIKISTAN

Dushanbe

0   60   120   180   miles

AFGHANISTAN   PAKISTAN

Armenia
Population: 3,330,000
Language: Armenian
Capital: Yerevan
Average person's buying power: $3,800

Azerbaijan
Population: 7,840,000
Language: Azerbaijani (Azeri)
Capital: Baku
Average person's buying power: $3,500

Georgia
Population: 4,940,000
Language: Georgian
Capital: Tbilisi
Average person's buying power: $3,100

Kazakhstan
Population: 16,770,000
Languages: Kazakh, Russian
Capital: Astana
Average person's buying power: $6,300

Kyrgyzstan
Population: 4,900,000
Languages: Kyrgyz, Russian
Capital: Bishkek
Average person's buying power: $2,800

Tajikistan
Population: 6,870,000
Languages: Tajik, Russian
Capital: Dushanbe
Average person's buying power: $1,250

Turkmenistan
Population: 4,780,000
Languages: Turkmen, Russian
Capital: Ashgabat
Average person's buying power: $5,500

Uzbekistan
Population: 25,990,000
Languages: Uzbek, Russian
Capital: Tashkent
Average person's buying power: $2,500

The Aral Sea is shrinking fast! This body of water lies between Uzbekistan and Kazakhstan. Today it covers one-third of the area it once did. Huge amounts of water have been drained to help water crops. So much has been taken that some ships have been left stranded and the once-important fishing industry has disappeared.

Iran

Iran has been around for a long, long time. Dating back almost 5,000 years, it is one of the oldest countries in the world! It has sometimes been called Persia.

Iran is an oil-rich country located in southwestern Asia. The Gulf of Oman borders it to the south. The Persian Gulf lies to the southwest. North of Iran are the Caspian Sea and former Soviet Asian countries.

Most of Iran lies on a plateau. It is one of the highest countries in the world. Much of central and eastern Iran is covered with desert. Villages are scattered around the deserts and in the mountains.

Have you ever been to a bazaar? In Iran, *bazaar* means "market." The city of Tehran has one of the biggest bazaars in the country. The bazaar here is hundreds of years old, but it stands next to modern buildings near the center of the city.

Carpet-Making Crafts

In Iran, sometimes a carpet makes up most of the furniture in a house! Iranians traditionally use the floor and the carpet for just about everything. They are used for sitting, sleeping, and praying. Because carpets are so important in Iran, they are handmade and absolutely beautiful.

Take a look at this carpet from Iran. What designs do you see? Common rug patterns include flowers, fruits, and animals. And the colors are so bright! The colors come from dyes produced from plants. Each region of Iran has its own unique colors and patterns.

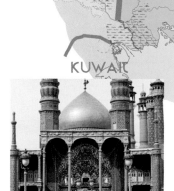

You know you have reached Qom when you see the golden dome. Qom is an ancient sacred city in central Iran. The golden-domed shrine located here is a tomb where saints are buried. Shiite Muslims travel here each year for religious holidays.

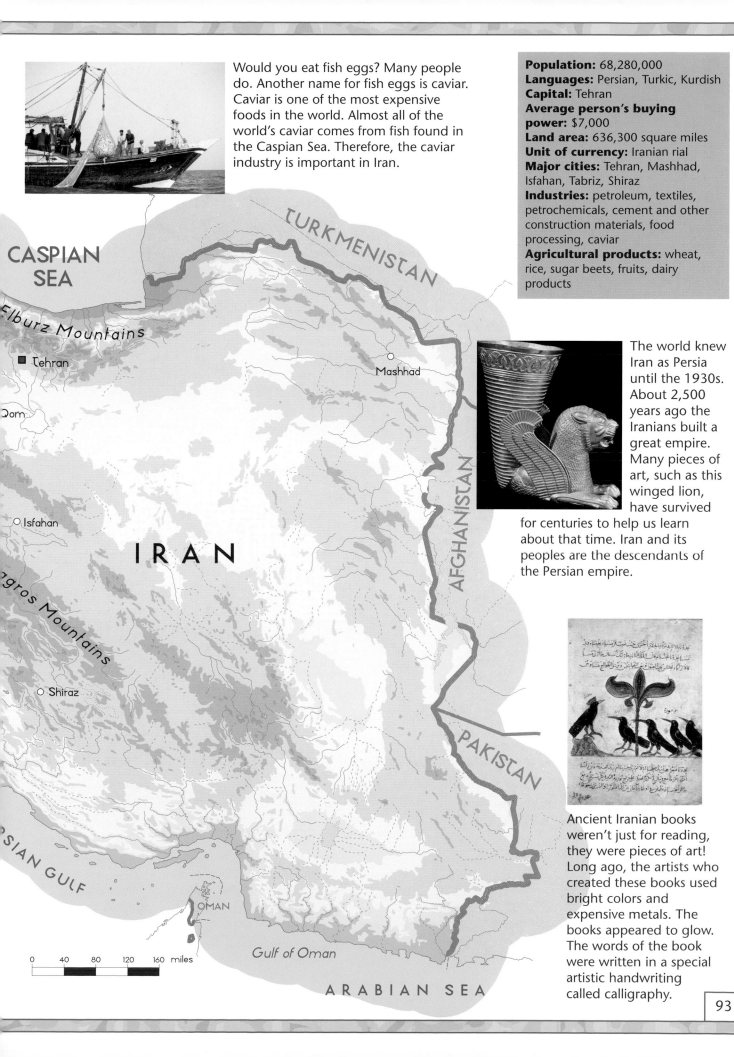

Would you eat fish eggs? Many people do. Another name for fish eggs is caviar. Caviar is one of the most expensive foods in the world. Almost all of the world's caviar comes from fish found in the Caspian Sea. Therefore, the caviar industry is important in Iran.

Population: 68,280,000
Languages: Persian, Turkic, Kurdish
Capital: Tehran
Average person's buying power: $7,000
Land area: 636,300 square miles
Unit of currency: Iranian rial
Major cities: Tehran, Mashhad, Isfahan, Tabriz, Shiraz
Industries: petroleum, textiles, petrochemicals, cement and other construction materials, food processing, caviar
Agricultural products: wheat, rice, sugar beets, fruits, dairy products

CASPIAN SEA

Elburz Mountains

Tehran

Qom

Mashhad

TURKMENISTAN

AFGHANISTAN

Isfahan

IRAN

Zagros Mountains

Shiraz

PAKISTAN

The world knew Iran as Persia until the 1930s. About 2,500 years ago the Iranians built a great empire. Many pieces of art, such as this winged lion, have survived for centuries to help us learn about that time. Iran and its peoples are the descendants of the Persian empire.

Ancient Iranian books weren't just for reading, they were pieces of art! Long ago, the artists who created these books used bright colors and expensive metals. The books appeared to glow. The words of the book were written in a special artistic handwriting called calligraphy.

PERSIAN GULF

OMAN

0   40   80   120   160 miles

Gulf of Oman

ARABIAN SEA

Turkey

Turkey lies in two continents. Part is located in Europe, while the rest lies in Asia. The culture in Turkey reflects the mix of continents. The European area is called Thrace. Turkey's largest city, Istanbul, lies in this area. The Asian section of Turkey covers a large peninsula called Anatolia or Asia Minor. Many great civilizations thrived here. Today, most of Turkey's people live in cities or towns.

Even though it is one country, Cyprus has two personalities. Turks and Greeks live in their own areas of the island. Turkish Cypriots claim they have a separate country, but only Turkey agrees with them.

The Bosporus, the Sea of Marmara, and the Dardanelles

In Turkey, you can tell where Asia ends and Europe begins. This is because three different bodies of water separate Thrace from Anatolia. These bodies of water are often called the Turkish Straits. A strait is a channel that connects two bodies of water. The Turkish Straits are the Bosporus, the Sea of Marmara, and the Dardanelles. They provide the only link between the Black Sea and the Mediterranean Sea. By having the Straits in its territory, Turkey can control how ships move between the two.

Today Greeks are a small part of Turkey's population. Greeks were in this country in ancient times, too. Evidence of this stands south of the city of Izmir. Here you can see ruins of an ancient Greek city called Ephesus. The Greeks founded many cities along the Mediterranean coast.

Turkey's rivers dry up over the hot, dry summers. But in spring, look out! Many rivers overflow as melting snow rushes down from the mountains. To control flooding, Turkey has built dams across the rivers. The dams also help water farmland and provide electric power.

Do you know the story of Noah's Ark? It is from the Bible. Noah built an ark, or boat, to save the animals from a great flood. According to some stories, Noah landed at Mount Ararat after the flood. Mount Ararat is the highest mountain in Turkey.

BLACK SEA

GEORGIA

Trabzon

ARMENIA

natolia

Ankara

TURKEY

Euphrates

Mt Ararat ▲

IRAN

Kayseri

Lake Van

Tigris

Adana

Euphrates

Tigris

IRAQ

SYRIA

0 30 60 90 miles

CYPRUS

osia

What is your favorite board game? In Turkey, backgammon and dominoes are popular. Backgammon is one of the world's oldest games. It has been played in this part of the world for centuries. Even today, many Turks spend their time in coffeehouses playing these ancient games.

The Kurds are a group of people who live in the mountainous regions of southeast Turkey. Their area also stretches over parts of Armenia, Iran, Iraq, and Syria. They have their own language and culture. Over the years they have fought for an independent Kurdish country.

Iraq

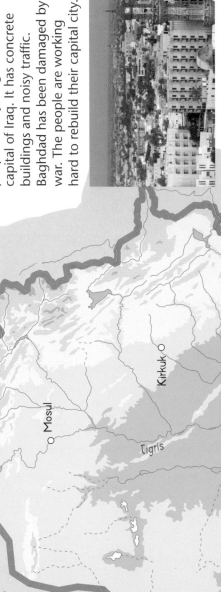

In ancient times, Baghdad was an important trading center. Camel caravans and crowded bazaars filled the city with people. Today, Baghdad is the capital of Iraq. It has concrete buildings and noisy traffic. Baghdad has been damaged by war. The people are working hard to rebuild their capital city.

You have probably heard of Iraq. It is a country in southwestern Asia. Iraq's history goes way back to ancient times. In fact, the world's first known civilization rose right here along the Tigris and Euphrates rivers. These rivers flow through the middle of Iraq toward the Persian Gulf. For thousands of years, people have relied on the rivers' water for drinking and farming. Beyond the river valleys lie vast areas of hot, dry desert. Some parts of Iraq have huge, underground oil fields. This oil is used throughout the world. Today, different groups of people live in Iraq. Arabs live in the southern and central parts of Iraq. Kurds live in the northern areas.

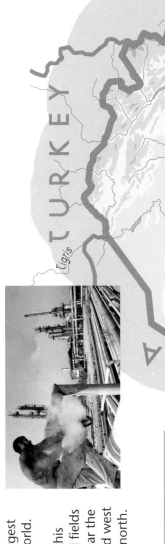

Iraq has the second-largest reserves of oil in the world. Oil has been a very important industry in this country. Iraq's main oil fields are in southern Iraq near the border with Kuwait and west of Kirkuk, a city in the north.

Population: 24,690,000
Languages: Arabic, Kurdish
Capital: Baghdad
Average person's buying power: $2,400
Land area: 168,750 square miles
Unit of currency: Iraqi dinar
Major cities: Baghdad, Mosul, Basrah
Industries: petroleum, chemicals, textiles, construction materials, food processing
Agricultural products: wheat, barley, rice, cattle, sheep

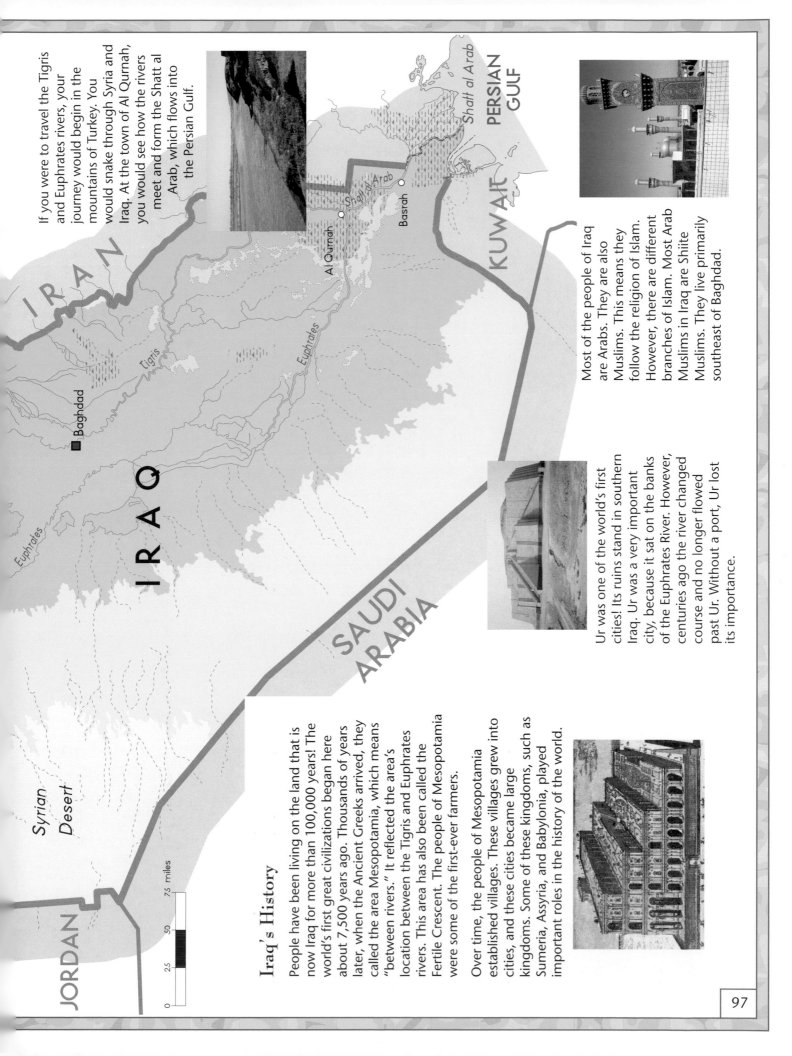

If you were to travel the Tigris and Euphrates rivers, your journey would begin in the mountains of Turkey. You would snake through Syria and Iraq. At the town of Al Qurnah, you would see how the rivers meet and form the Shatt al Arab, which flows into the Persian Gulf.

JORDAN

Syrian Desert

0   25   50   75 miles

IRAQ

Euphrates

Baghdad

Tigris

Euphrates

IRAN

Al Qurnah

Shatt al Arab

Basrah

Shatt al Arab

PERSIAN GULF

KUWAIT

SAUDI ARABIA

Iraq's History

People have been living on the land that is now Iraq for more than 100,000 years! The world's first great civilizations began here about 7,500 years ago. Thousands of years later, when the Ancient Greeks arrived, they called the area Mesopotamia, which means "between rivers." It reflected the area's location between the Tigris and Euphrates rivers. This area has also been called the Fertile Crescent. The people of Mesopotamia were some of the first-ever farmers.

Over time, the people of Mesopotamia established villages. These villages grew into cities, and these cities became large kingdoms. Some of these kingdoms, such as Sumeria, Assyria, and Babylonia, played important roles in the history of the world.

Ur was one of the world's first cities! Its ruins stand in southern Iraq. Ur was a very important city, because it sat on the banks of the Euphrates River. However, centuries ago the river changed course and no longer flowed past Ur. Without a port, Ur lost its importance.

Most of the people of Iraq are Arabs. They are also Muslims. This means they follow the religion of Islam. However, there are different branches of Islam. Most Arab Muslims in Iraq are Shiite Muslims. They live primarily southeast of Baghdad.

The Middle East

The Middle East is an area covered with desert. But the land here isn't completely dry. There is a liquid that flows underground, but you can't drink it. That liquid is oil. Thanks to this "black gold," Middle Eastern countries can afford to build modern cities, royal palaces, hospitals, and airports. Not everyone benefits from oil, however. Countries such as Jordan and Yemen do not have as much oil and are poorer than their neighbors. In the past, people were herders or farmers. Nowadays, most people in the Middle East live in cities.

Imagine living in a house of solid stone! Petra, a city in Jordan, was carved out of sandstone rock thousands of years ago. It became a successful trading city, but for centuries it was almost deserted. Although people in Jordan always knew about it, Westerners rediscovered it in the early 1800s.

Bahrain
Population: 670,000
Languages: Arabic, English
Capital: Manama
Average person's buying power: $14,000

Jordan
Population: 5,470,000
Language: Arabic
Capital: Amman
Average person's buying power: $4,300

Kuwait
Population: 2,190,000
Languages: Arabic, English
Capital: Kuwait
Average person's buying power: $15,000

Lebanon
Population: 3,730,000
Language: Arabic
Capital: Beirut
Average person's buying power: $5,400

Oman
Population: 2,810,000
Language: Arabic
Capital: Muscat
Average person's buying power: $8,300

Qatar
Population: 820,000
Languages: Arabic, English
Capital: Doha
Average person's buying power: $21,500

Saudi Arabia
Population: 24,300,000
Language: Arabic
Capital: Riyadh
Average person's buying power: $10,500

Syria
Population: 17,590,000
Languages: Arabic, Kurdish
Capital: Damascus
Average person's buying power: $3,500

United Arab Emirates
Population: 2,490,000
Languages: Arabic, Persian, English, Hindi
Capital: Abu Dhabi
Average person's buying power: $22,000

Yemen
Population: 19,350,000
Language: Arabic
Capital: Sanaa
Average person's buying power: $840

MEDITERRANEAN SEA

SYRI

LEBANON
Beirut

Damascus

ISRAEL

Amman

EGYPT

JORDAN
Petra

Gulf of Suez

Gulf of Aqaba

EGYPT

Medina

RED SEA

Mecca

SUDAN

ERITREA

ETHIOPIA

0   50   100   150 miles

DJIB

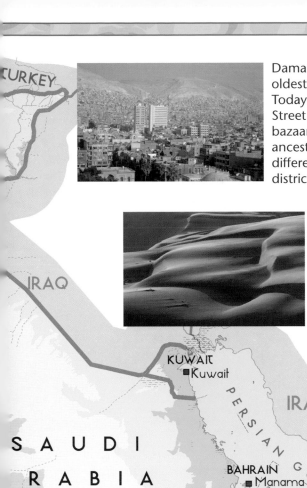

Damascus is Syria's capital. It is the oldest capital city in the world. Today it offers a mix of old and new. Street merchants sell their goods in bazaars called *suqs,* just as their ancestors did. This area is very different from the main business district, which has modern buildings.

The desert has some interesting landscapes. Ergs are areas of ever-changing sand dunes. Wadis are hard, dry valleys where water gathers if it ever rains. Oases are fertile areas with water. You might think there are no plants here, but the date palm tree grows well in dry places.

Mecca

Mecca is a city in western Saudi Arabia where the prophet Muhammad, the founder of Islam, was born. Mecca is Islam's holiest place. Every year millions of people flock to the city. Muslims come from all over the world during this pilgrimage known as the hajj. It is the dream of every Muslim to make this trip at least once.

In the center of the Great Mosque in this city, there is a small square building called the Kaaba. Set into one corner is the Black Stone. Muslims the world over turn toward it when they pray.

When you see a woman dressed like this, chances are she is from the Middle East. It is the custom for Muslim women to be fully covered. Many wear long robes and veils. Some traditional Muslim women live in seclusion, away from men.

Have you tasted salt water? It's pretty yucky. Salty seawater is not suitable for drinking or watering crops. But in areas of the Middle East, that is the only water around. There is a way to remove the salt from the water, but it costs a lot. Factories have been built to do this job in wealthy countries.

Israel, West Bank, and Gaza Strip

ילדה –
Hebrew girl

ولد
Arabic boy

As you read this book, you are reading the words from left to right. But if you were to read Hebrew or Arabic, you would read from right to left. Do you think it would be hard to learn to read and write a different way?

Israel is on the Mediterranean Sea. The area known as Palestine includes the West Bank and the Gaza Strip. Israel currently controls these areas, but the Israelis and Palestinian Arabs are working on ending their long conflict.

Long ago, this land was the homeland of the Jews. The Romans took over and called the area Palestine. Many Jews left. Over the centuries, different nations controlled the land. When the United Kingdom won control, many Jews returned. In 1948, the nation of Israel was established for them. But Israel was immediately attacked by some Arab nations unhappy about the new country. Israel has fought several wars with Arab nations.

Tel Aviv offers a bit of everything. Stretched along the sandy beaches of the Mediterranean, this is Israel's most modern city. It is also the country's cultural center, with museums, galleries, and theaters.

The Holy Land is the setting for many stories in the Bible. And much of the Holy Land is located in the area called the West Bank. For example, Bethlehem, the birthplace of Jesus Christ, is here. The Church of the Nativity, shown here, is said to have been built on that very spot.

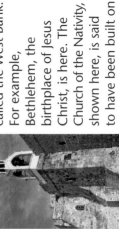

LEBANON

GOLAN HEIGHTS
Claimed by Israel and Syria

SYRIA

Jordan

Nazareth

Jordan

Haifa

WEST

MEDITERRANEAN SEA

Tel Aviv

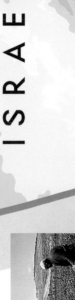

The Dead Sea is actually a lake! Its shore lies about 1,310 feet below sea level, making it the lowest place on earth. It is about nine times saltier than the ocean. That makes it impossible for plants or animals to live in the water. That's where it gets its name.

Israel

Population: 6,120,000
Languages: Hebrew, Arabic, English
Capitals: Tel Aviv and Jerusalem
Average person's buying power: $19,000
Land area: 8,020 square miles
Unit of currency: new Israeli shekel
Major cities: Jerusalem, Tel Aviv, Haifa
Industries: high-technology projects, wood and paper products, potash and phosphates, food, beverages
Agricultural products: citrus, vegetables, cotton, beef, poultry

Gaza Strip

Population: 1,280,000
Languages: Arabic, Hebrew
Average person's buying power: $600
Land area: 140 square miles

West Bank

Population: 2,240,000
Languages: Arabic, Hebrew
Average person's buying power: $800
Land area: 2,260 square miles

WEST BANK AND GAZA STRIP
territories claimed by Palestinian Authority

GAZA STRIP

0   9   18   27 miles

Palestinians, such as this farmer, do not have their own nation, but they want to create one. The Palestinian Authority has established many elements of independence, such as a system of laws and an elected president and prime minister. But continuing violence from both sides makes it difficult for Palestinians and Israelis to agree.

Jerusalem

Jerusalem is a holy city for three faiths: Judaism, Islam, and Christianity. Western Jerusalem is modern with high-rise buildings. Eastern Jerusalem is home to the old holy city. This is where Jews worship at the 2,000-year-old Western Wall, one of the holiest Jewish sites. Behind it stands the Dome of the Rock, the Muslim mosque built at the place where the prophet Muhammad is said to have ridden a winged horse into heaven. Many events in the life of Jesus Christ also took place in Jerusalem. Israel makes its capital here, but most other countries treat Tel Aviv as Israel's capital.

JORDAN

Dead Sea

Bethlehem

BANK

Beersheba

ISRAEL

Negev

EGYPT

SAUDI ARABIA

Gulf of Aqaba

Africa

Think about Africa. What comes to your mind? You probably picture large wild animals roaming large areas of grassland. Maybe you think of dark jungle. You might even imagine ferocious lions hunting herds of zebra. But Africa is home to much more than lions, zebras, and other wild animals. It is also a land of very diverse people.

More than 800 ethnic groups call Africa their home. Each group speaks its own language, has its own beliefs, and follows its own way of life. Nearly every African country has many languages.

The second-largest continent in area, Africa lies between the Atlantic and Indian Oceans and the Mediterranean Sea. It covers about one-fifth of the earth's land area. Huge deserts, such as the Sahara and Kalahari Desert, make up a good portion of this land. The Sahara alone covers nearly one-third of Africa's land, spreading across an area almost as big as the United States. Tropical rain forests grow in western and central Africa. This continent is also home to the world's longest river—the Nile.

Africa's population also ranks second among the continents. Only Asia has more people. A good portion of the population is young. Almost half of Africa's people are under the age of 15.

EUROPE

NORTH ATLANTIC OCEAN

MOROCCO

ALGERIA

WESTERN SAHARA (claimed by Morocco)

MAURITANIA

CAPE VERDE

SENEGAL

THE GAMBIA

GUINEA-BISSAU

GUINEA

M A

BURKINA FASO

BENIN

GHANA

SIERRA LEONE

CÔTE D'IVOIRE

LIBERIA

TOGO

SÃO TOMÉ AND PRINCIPE

EQUATORIAL GUINEA

SOUTH ATLANTIC OCEAN

0   300   600   900   miles

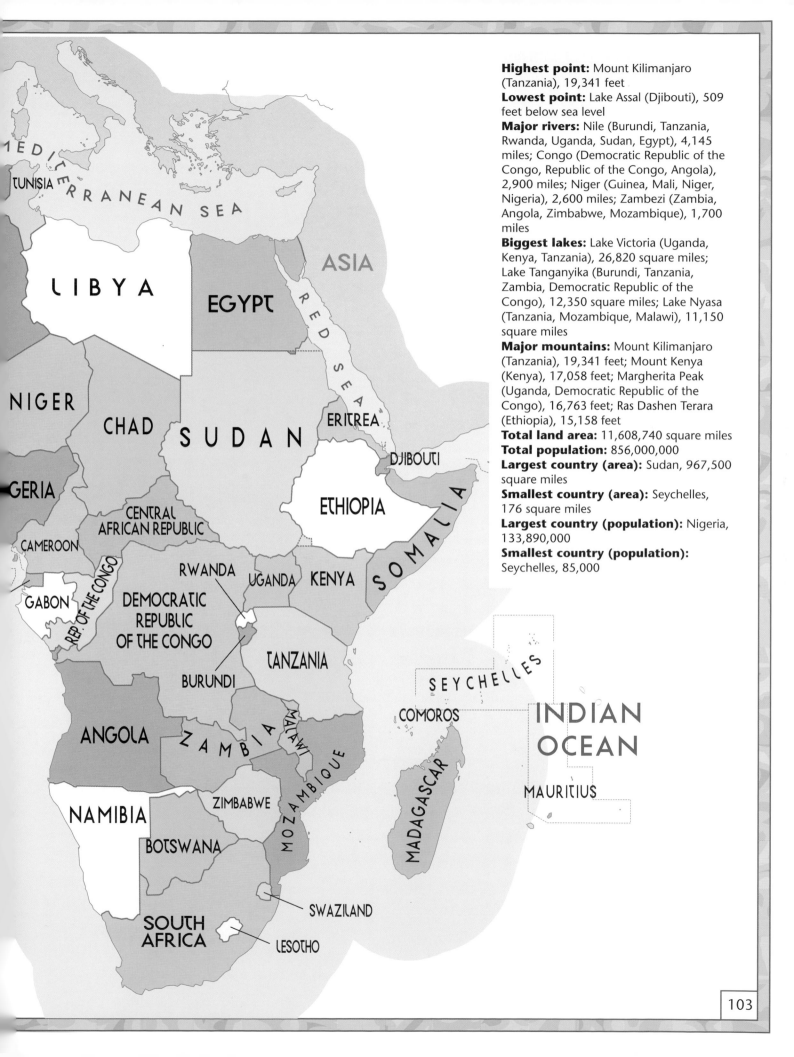

Highest point: Mount Kilimanjaro (Tanzania), 19,341 feet

Lowest point: Lake Assal (Djibouti), 509 feet below sea level

Major rivers: Nile (Burundi, Tanzania, Rwanda, Uganda, Sudan, Egypt), 4,145 miles; Congo (Democratic Republic of the Congo, Republic of the Congo, Angola), 2,900 miles; Niger (Guinea, Mali, Niger, Nigeria), 2,600 miles; Zambezi (Zambia, Angola, Zimbabwe, Mozambique), 1,700 miles

Biggest lakes: Lake Victoria (Uganda, Kenya, Tanzania), 26,820 square miles; Lake Tanganyika (Burundi, Tanzania, Zambia, Democratic Republic of the Congo), 12,350 square miles; Lake Nyasa (Tanzania, Mozambique, Malawi), 11,150 square miles

Major mountains: Mount Kilimanjaro (Tanzania), 19,341 feet; Mount Kenya (Kenya), 17,058 feet; Margherita Peak (Uganda, Democratic Republic of the Congo), 16,763 feet; Ras Dashen Terara (Ethiopia), 15,158 feet

Total land area: 11,608,740 square miles

Total population: 856,000,000

Largest country (area): Sudan, 967,500 square miles

Smallest country (area): Seychelles, 176 square miles

Largest country (population): Nigeria, 133,890,000

Smallest country (population): Seychelles, 85,000

North Africa

Can you ski in Africa? Yes, you can. The snow-capped Atlas Mountains offer a contrast to the desert. They rise in northwest Africa and separate the moist northern climate from the dry south. The slopes facing north have farmland and forests. Those facing south have mostly grasslands.

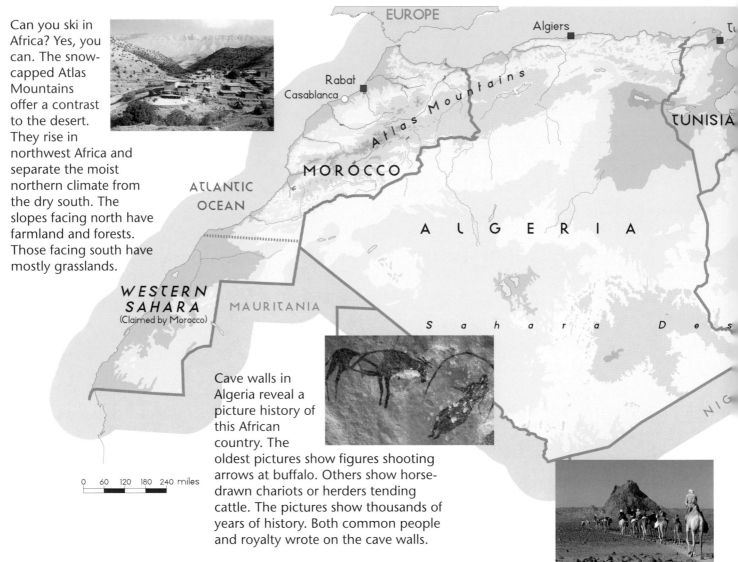

Cave walls in Algeria reveal a picture history of this African country. The oldest pictures show figures shooting arrows at buffalo. Others show horse-drawn chariots or herders tending cattle. The pictures show thousands of years of history. Both common people and royalty wrote on the cave walls.

You can't see his face. He is wearing blue robes and a white turban on his head. Who is he? He is a Tuareg. The Tuaregs are a nomadic people. They roam the Sahara looking for water and pastureland. Most ride camels, although nowadays many travel by truck.

If you're planning a trip to North Africa, bring lots of water. It's a hot and dry place. Most of the land is covered with sandy desert. Egypt's Western Desert covers more than half the country.

The Nile River flows across Egypt. People have farmed the Nile Valley for thousands of years. It is one of the most heavily populated places on earth. Most people in North Africa are Arab.

The Arabs call Morocco *Maghreb,* which means "the west." The Maghreb region now includes the countries of Algeria and Tunisia, and the territory of Western Sahara as well.

The Pyramids and the Sphinx

Look at these giant triangles! Actually, they are pyramids. The ancient Egyptians built these pyramids. Thousands of years ago, kings called pharaohs ruled the land. They were very rich. When a pharaoh died, he was buried in a giant tomb, or grave. The tomb was hidden inside these huge stone pyramids. Some are as high as a ten-story building! Sitting with the pyramids is a statue of a sphinx, a lion with a man's head. This statue may have been meant to protect the pyramids.

Egypt would be a desert wasteland were it not for the Nile, the longest river in the world. The Nile Valley and Delta are areas of rich farmland surrounded by dry land. Egypt's capital, Cairo, sits on both sides of the Nile.

When you shop, you probably stop at many stores to get everything you need. In North Africa, you can do all your shopping in one stop: the marketplace, or bazaar. Markets are also an important meeting place. People come to trade not only goods, but daily news as well.

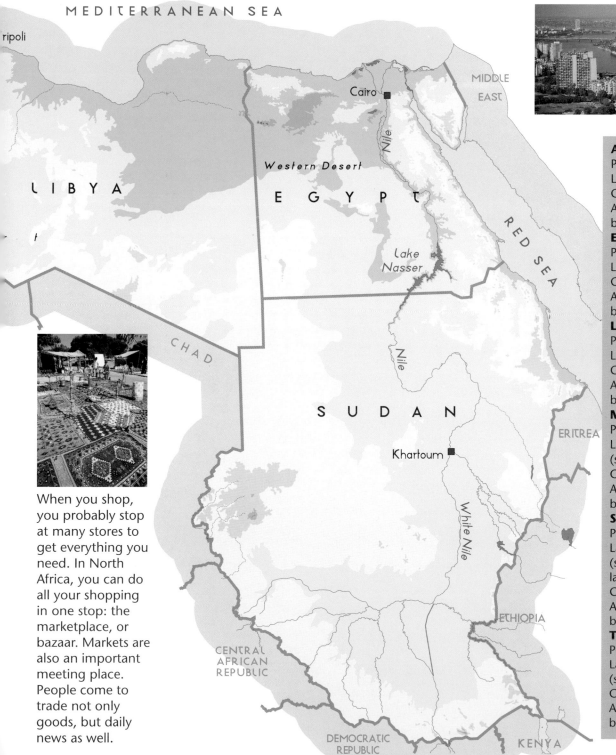

Algeria
Population: 32,820,000
Language: Arabic
Capital: Algiers
Average person's buying power: $5,300

Egypt
Population: 74,720,000
Language: Arabic
Capital: Cairo
Average person's buying power: $3,900

Libya
Population: 5,500,000
Language: Arabic
Capital: Tripoli
Average person's buying power: $7,600

Morocco
Population: 31,690,000
Language: Arabic (some Berber dialects)
Capital: Rabat
Average person's buying power: $3,900

Sudan
Population: 38,120,000
Language: Arabic (some Nubian, other languages in south)
Capital: Khartoum
Average person's buying power: $1,420

Tunisia
Population: 9,930,000
Language: Arabic (some French)
Capital: Tunis
Average person's buying power: $6,500

West Africa

Ready to enjoy the Atlantic coast in West Africa? You can take your pick of countries to visit, from Mauritania to Benin. And there are more countries to see inland. The northern areas of this area are hot and dry. But move south, and things get much wetter and greener. Parts of this area are very wet—more than 150 inches of rain falls each year! This moisture is what keeps the Guinea coast covered in tropical forest.

While you are visiting West Africa, get to know some of the hundreds of different ethnic groups who make their home here.

Many West African countries grow crops to sell to other countries. These crops include coffee, cocoa, peanuts, cotton, and fruit. However, growing crops to feed themselves is also important to many African farmers. Millet is a grain many grow. Certain kinds of millet grow well in droughts.

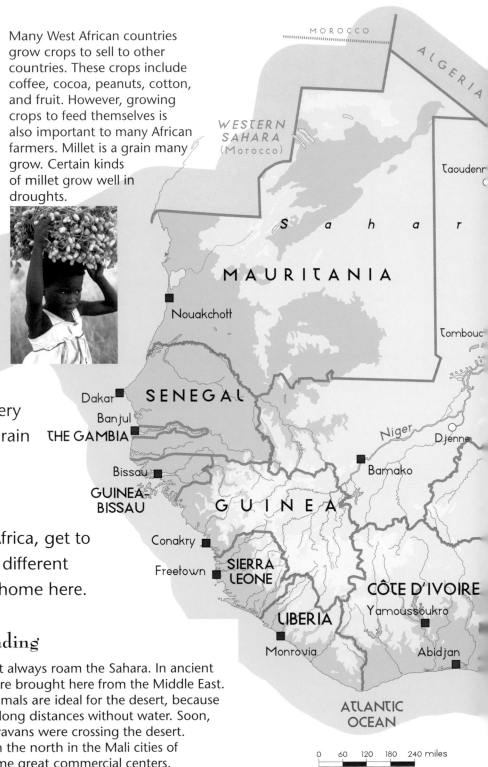

Sahara Trading

Camels did not always roam the Sahara. In ancient times, they were brought here from the Middle East. These pack animals are ideal for the desert, because they can walk long distances without water. Soon, long camel caravans were crossing the desert. Traders from the south met traders from the north in the Mali cities of Tombouctou and Gao. Both cities became great commercial centers.

Caravans from the north brought cowrie shells to use as money. They also carried salt, which was sometimes used as money. Merchants from the south traded gold, ivory, and kola nuts.

These mounds of salt come from Senegal's Rose Lake. People take water from the lake. When it evaporates, it leaves a lot of salt behind. Taoudenni, Mali, has salt mines, where people take salt from the ground. Salt was once very precious, worth as much as gold!

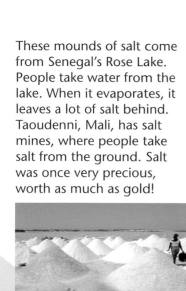

Look at the colors in this fabric! This is the work of the Asante, an ethnic group of Ghana. It is called Kente cloth. When the cloth was first made, only Asante royalty could wear it. Now the brilliant patterns of Kente cloth are popular with many people.

Benin
Population: 7,050,000
Language: French (some Fon, Yoruba)
Capitals: Porto-Novo and Cotonou
Average person's buying power: $1,070

Burkina Faso
Population: 13,230,000
Language: French (some Moore, Jula)
Capital: Ouagadougou
Average person's buying power: $1,080

Cape Verde
Population: 420,000
Language: Portuguese (some Portuguese Creole)
Capital: Praia
Average person's buying power: $1,400

Côte d'Ivoire (Ivory Coast)
Population: 16,970,000
Language: French (some Dioula)
Capitals: Yamoussoukro and Abidjan
Average person's buying power: $1,500

The Gambia
Population: 1,510,000
Language: English (some Mandinka, Wolof, Fula)
Capital: Banjul
Average person's buying power: $1,800

Ghana
Population: 20,470,000
Language: English (some Akan, Moshi-Dagomba, Ewe, Ga)
Capital: Accra
Average person's buying power: $2,100

Guinea
Population: 9,040,000
Language: French (some Fuuta-Jalon)
Capital: Conakry
Average person's buying power: $2,000

Guinea–Bissau
Population: 1,370,000
Language: Portuguese (some Portuguese Creole)
Capital: Bissau
Average person's buying power: $800

Liberia
Population: 3,320,000
Language: English (more than 20 different tribal languages)
Capital: Monrovia
Average person's buying power: $1,100

Mali
Population: 11,630,000
Languages: French, Bambara
Capital: Bamako
Average person's buying power: $860

Mauritania
Population: 2,920,000
Languages: Arabic, Wolof (some Pulaar, Soninke)
Capital: Nouakchott
Average person's buying power: $1,900

Niger
Population: 11,060,000
Language: French (some Hausa, Djerma)
Capital: Niamey
Average person's buying power: $830

Senegal
Population: 10,590,000
Language: French (some Wolof, Pulaar, Dioula, Mandinka)
Capital: Dakar
Average person's buying power: $1,500

Sierra Leone
Population: 5,740,000
Languages: English, Mende, Temne (some Krio)
Capital: Freetown
Average person's buying power: $580

Togo
Population: 5,430,000
Language: French (some Ewe, Mina, Kabye, Dagomba)
Capital: Lomé
Average person's buying power: $1,500

What would life be like if you lived in West Africa? If there were a school near you, you would go to school. After school, you might play soccer or a board game called mankala. You would also help your family around the house and farm.

This mosque in Djenne, Mali, is made of mud! Called the Great Mosque, it is similar to all Islamic mosques in many ways. However, the mud makes it unique to Djenne, where there are many mud structures. Each spring, people gather together to repair any damage caused by rain.

Nigeria

What is the giant of Africa? Is it a ferocious animal, such as an elephant or lion? Is it a huge structure? Actually, the giant of Africa is Africa's most populated country. It is Nigeria.

Nigeria sits south of the Sahara. It is a land of rushing rivers, lush rain forests, spectacular mountain scenery, hot swamplands, and wide-open grasslands. It also has many different kinds of people. More than 250 ethnic groups live here. They speak more than 200 languages and have many religions. Most Nigerians live in rural areas. But this giant of Africa is also home to many large cities.

The Yoruba are an ethnic group that live in Nigeria. They are famous for the crafts they make. These include elaborately carved wooden masks. The Yoruba also work with bronze metal. They trade their pieces of art at marketplaces.

BENIN

Kaduna

Niger

Abuja

Ibadan

Lagos

ATLANTIC OCEAN

Niger

Niger Delta

Population: 133,890,000
Language: English (some Hausa, Yoruba, Igbo, Fulani, many others)
Capital: Abuja
Average person's buying power: $875
Land area: 356,670 square miles
Unit of currency: naira
Major cities: Lagos, Ibadan, Kano, Kaduna
Industries: crude oil, coal, tin, columbite, rubber
Agricultural products: cocoa, peanuts, palm oil, cattle, timber

If you like the hustle and bustle of the city, take a trip to Lagos! This is Nigeria's largest city. It was built on a series of islands surrounded by lagoons. Lagos used to be the capital of Nigeria. It is still the country's main business center.

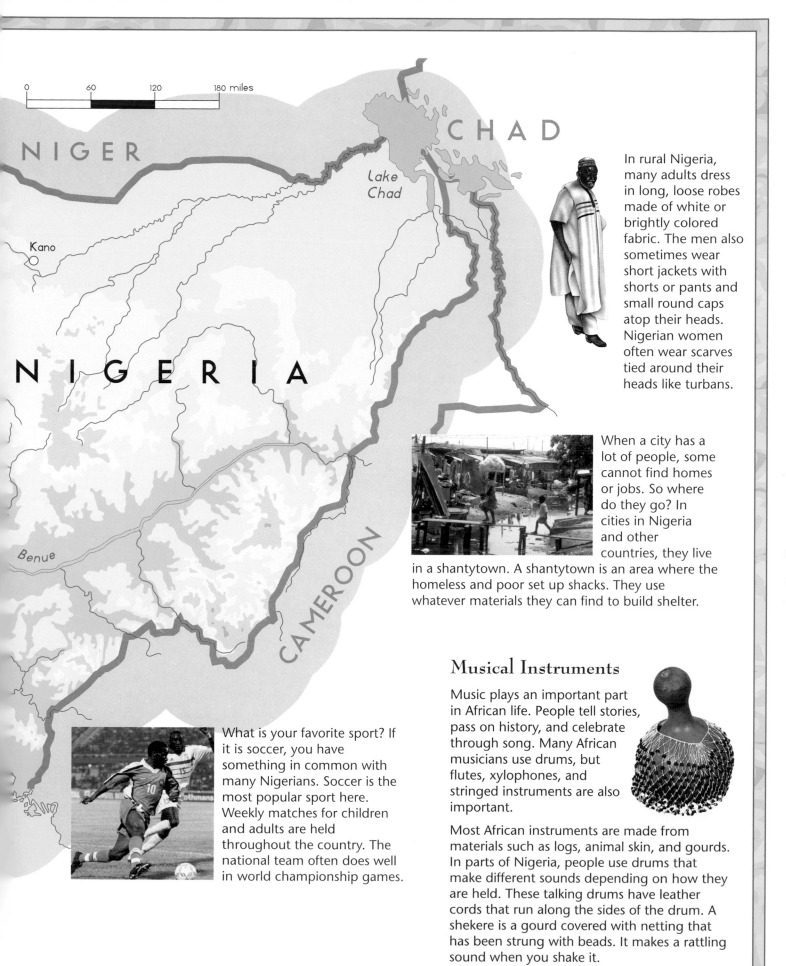

In rural Nigeria, many adults dress in long, loose robes made of white or brightly colored fabric. The men also sometimes wear short jackets with shorts or pants and small round caps atop their heads. Nigerian women often wear scarves tied around their heads like turbans.

When a city has a lot of people, some cannot find homes or jobs. So where do they go? In cities in Nigeria and other countries, they live in a shantytown. A shantytown is an area where the homeless and poor set up shacks. They use whatever materials they can find to build shelter.

What is your favorite sport? If it is soccer, you have something in common with many Nigerians. Soccer is the most popular sport here. Weekly matches for children and adults are held throughout the country. The national team often does well in world championship games.

Musical Instruments

Music plays an important part in African life. People tell stories, pass on history, and celebrate through song. Many African musicians use drums, but flutes, xylophones, and stringed instruments are also important.

Most African instruments are made from materials such as logs, animal skin, and gourds. In parts of Nigeria, people use drums that make different sounds depending on how they are held. These talking drums have leather cords that run along the sides of the drum. A shekere is a gourd covered with netting that has been strung with beads. It makes a rattling sound when you shake it.

Central Africa

Much of the heart of Africa is covered with rain forest. This is where the greenest parts of the continent lie. In fact, Africa's largest tropical rain forest is found here. It is also the second-largest rain forest on earth. It stretches into Gabon, the Congo River basin, and the Central African Republic. While Cameroon has a mix of landscapes, its southern area is also covered with rain forest. Chad has a dryer landscape. The country of Equatorial Guinea is divided between the African mainland and islands. São Tomé and Principe is made up of islands off the coast of Africa.

Look out overhead! A hornbill is flying among the treetops in search of fruit. This bird looks a lot like a toucan. It uses its large beak to crack nuts. The African rain forests are home to all kinds of birds and animals.

Think about the animals you visit at the zoo. How many come from Africa? Chimpanzees do. The African elephant is the world's largest elephant. Other large animals from Africa include rhinoceroses and hippopotamuses. Crocodiles can also be found here.

Cameroon
Population: 15,750,000
Languages: English, French, 24 major African language groups
Capital: Yaoundé
Average person's buying power: $1,700

Central African Republic
Population: 3,690,000
Languages: French, Sangho, more than ten major tribal languages
Capital: Bangui
Average person's buying power: $1,300

Chad
Population: 9,260,000
Languages: French, Arabic, Sara
Capital: N'Djamena
Average person's buying power: $1,100

Democratic Republic of the Congo
Population: 56,630,000
Languages: French, Lingala, Kingwana, Kikongo, Tshiluba
Capital: Kinshasa
Average person's buying power: $610

Equatorial Guinea
Population: 520,000
Languages: Spanish, French, Fang, Bubi
Capital: Malabo
Average person's buying power: $2,700

Gabon
Population: 1,330,000
Languages: French, Fang, Myeni, Nzebi, Bapounou/Eschira, Bandjabi
Capital: Libreville
Average person's buying power: $5,700

Republic of the Congo
Population: 2,960,000
Languages: French, Lingala, Monokutuba, Kikongo
Capital: Brazzaville
Average person's buying power: $900

São Tomé and Principe
Population: 180,000
Language: Portuguese
Capital: São Tomé
Average person's buying power: $1,200

LIBYA

NIGER

NIGERIA

CHAD

N'Djamena

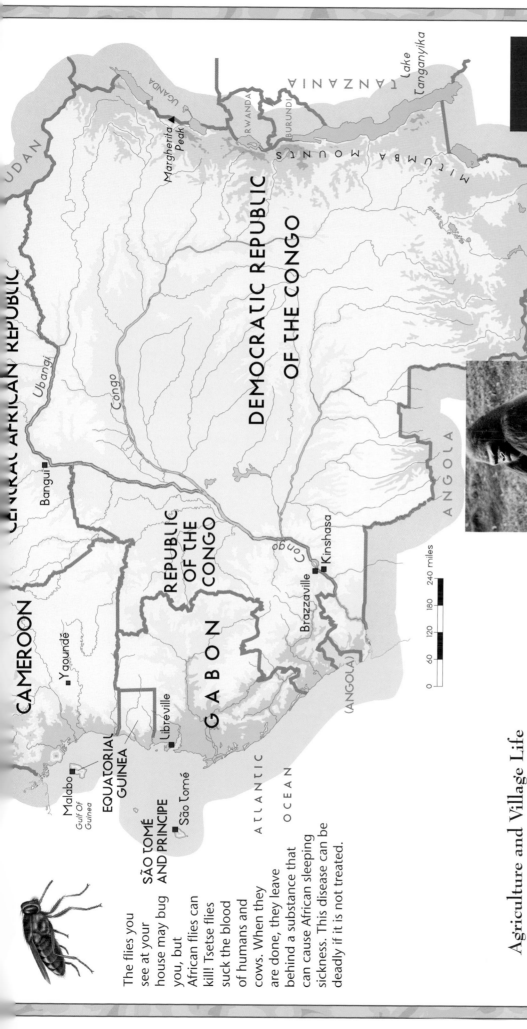

CAMEROON

CENTRAL AFRICAN REPUBLIC

SUDAN

UGANDA

Margherita Peak

RWANDA

BURUNDI

Lake Tanganyika

TANZANIA

MITUMBA MOUNTS

ZAMBIA

DEMOCRATIC REPUBLIC OF THE CONGO

Ubangi

Congo

Bangui

Yaoundé

REPUBLIC OF THE CONGO

GABON

Libreville

Kinshasa

Congo

Brazzaville

(ANGOLA)

ANGOLA

EQUATORIAL GUINEA

Malabo

Gulf Of Guinea

SÃO TOMÉ AND PRINCIPE

São Tomé

ATLANTIC OCEAN

0   60   120   180   240 miles

The flies you see at your house may bug you, but African flies can kill! Tsetse flies suck the blood of humans and cows. When they are done, they leave behind a substance that can cause African sleeping sickness. This disease can be deadly if it is not treated.

Over time, these four colors have come to represent Africa and African heritage. Many African nations use some or all of these colors in their flags. Red symbolizes blood. Black stands for the African people. Green represents the land of Africa. Yellow, or gold, symbolizes the wealth of the land.

Gorillas may be Africa's most famous animals. Lowland gorillas live in the lowland rain forests. They live and travel in packs, or families. They eat the plants and berries of the forest. Although some movies have shown gorillas as mean animals, they are actually shy and peaceful.

Agriculture and Village Life

Would you want to live in a city or a village? Most Africans south of the Sahara live in villages. Some villages are quite small, with only 40 to 50 people. Others are much bigger. Each village is a community of people belonging to the same ethnic group. In fact, in most villages, everyone is related. Village houses are usually clustered together and surrounded by farmland. Most African villagers farm the land and raise some animals. Most farm families grow food crops for their own use. Many also grow crops to sell or trade.

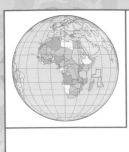

East Africa

East Africa is a land of mountains and lakes. Most of Africa's large lakes are found here, in the Great Rift Valley. Some are so shallow and salty that they are unsuitable for most life. They are called "Africa's Great Lakes." Other freshwater lakes provide a home to hundreds of kinds of fish. Lake Victoria is Africa's largest lake. This is where the Nile River begins.

Towering over East Africa is Mount Kilimanjaro. This snow-capped volcano is the highest mountain in Africa. The next-largest mountain is Mount Kenya. Volcanoes built these mountains higher and higher as they spewed out lava long ago.

Elephants, cheetahs, and lions roam East Africa's savannas. A savanna is an area of wide, grassy plains. Giraffes, ostriches, antelope, and zebras live here, too. Many live safely in national parks and wildlife reserves. People can go on a trip called a safari to see these animals up close.

Great Lakes and Rift Valley

Africa has a huge scar. That's what some people call the Great Rift Valley. It is actually a long, deep depression that crosses through the eastern half of the continent. Much of this depression is filled with water in the form of lakes.

The Great Rift Valley has two arms: eastern and western. The western branch runs along the border between the Democratic Republic of the Congo and Uganda, Rwanda, Burundi, and Tanzania. The eastern branch runs through Eritrea, Ethiopia, Kenya, and Tanzania. Some of the earliest-known human fossils have been found here.

RED SEA

Gulf of Aden

SOMALIA

ERITREA

Asmara

Lake Assal
Djibouti
DJIBOUTI

Ras Dashen Terara

ETHIOPIA

Addis Ababa

Blue Nile

Blue Nile

SUDAN

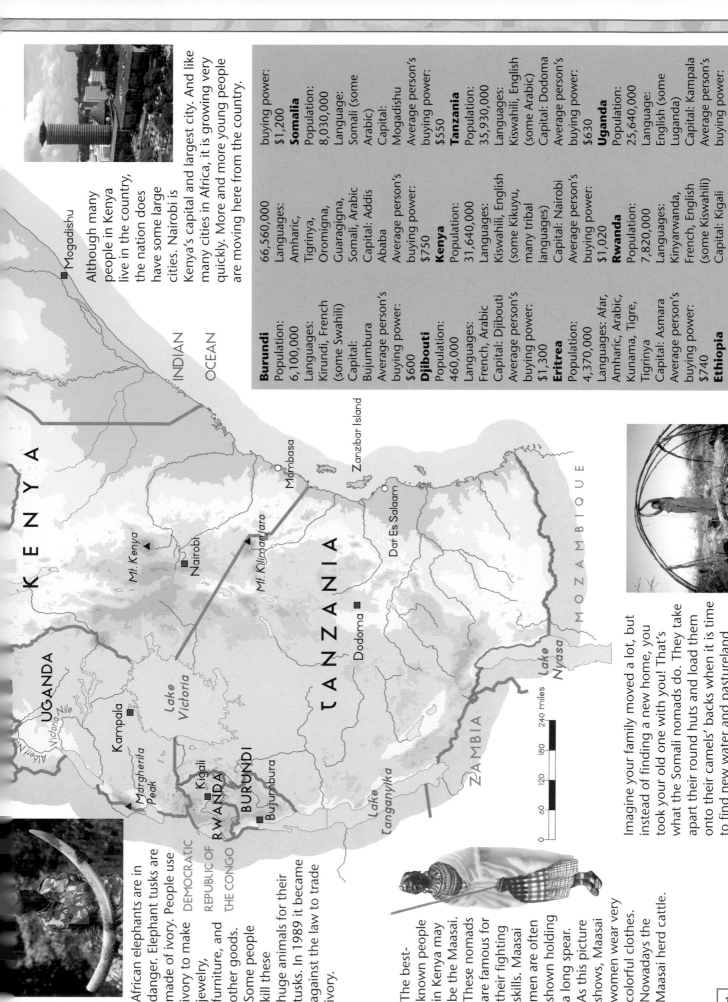

Although many people in Kenya live in the country, the nation does have some large cities. Nairobi is Kenya's capital and largest city. And like many cities in Africa, it is growing very quickly. More and more young people are moving here from the country.

Burundi
Population: 6,100,000
Languages: Kirundi, French (some Swahili)
Capital: Bujumbura
Average person's buying power: $600

Djibouti
Population: 460,000
Languages: French, Arabic
Capital: Djibouti
Average person's buying power: $1,300

Eritrea
Population: 4,370,000
Languages: Afar, Amharic, Arabic, Kunama, Tigre, Tigrinya
Capital: Asmara
Average person's buying power: $740

Ethiopia
Population: 66,560,000
Languages: Amharic, Tigrinya, Oromigna, Guaragigna, Somali, Arabic
Capital: Addis Ababa
Average person's buying power: $750

Kenya
Population: 31,640,000
Languages: Kiswahili, English (some Kikuyu, many tribal languages)
Capital: Nairobi
Average person's buying power: $1,020

Rwanda
Population: 7,820,000
Languages: Kinyarwanda, French, English (some Kiswahili)
Capital: Kigali
Average person's buying power: $1,200

Somalia
Population: 8,030,000
Language: Somali (some Arabic)
Capital: Mogadishu
Average person's buying power: $550

Tanzania
Population: 35,930,000
Languages: Kiswahili, English (some Arabic)
Capital: Dodoma
Average person's buying power: $630

Uganda
Population: 25,640,000
Language: English (some Luganda)
Capital: Kampala
Average person's buying power: $1,260

INDIAN OCEAN

Mogadishu

Mombasa

Zanzibar Island

Dar Es Salaam

K E N Y A

Mt. Kenya

Nairobi

Mt. Kilimanjaro

T A N Z A N I A

Dodoma

Lake Victoria

UGANDA

Kampala

Margherita Peak

Victoria Nile

Albert Nile

DEMOCRATIC REPUBLIC OF THE CONGO

R W A N D A

Kigali

BURUNDI

Bujumbura

Lake Tanganyika

ZAMBIA

Lake Nyasa

M O Z A M B I Q U E

0   60   120   180   240 miles

African elephants are in danger. Elephant tusks are made of ivory. People use ivory to make jewelry, furniture, and other goods. Some people kill these huge animals for their tusks. In 1989 it became against the law to trade ivory.

The best-known people in Kenya may be the Maasai. These nomads are famous for their fighting skills. Maasai men are often shown holding a long spear. As this picture shows, Maasai women wear very colorful clothes. Nowadays the Maasai herd cattle.

Imagine your family moved a lot, but instead of finding a new home, you took your old one with you! That's what the Somali nomads do. They take apart their round huts and load them onto their camels' backs when it is time to find new water and pastureland.

113

Southern Africa

The local name of Victoria Falls is *Mosi-oa-Tunya*. That means "the smoke that thunders." The Zambezi River spills over a long cliff on the border between Zimbabwe and Zambia. It creates a deafening roar and a cloud of spray that can be seen from miles away!

From the southern end of the Rift Valley, high grasslands grow. This area is known as the dry savanna. It spreads across the countries of Southern Africa. The dry savanna is home for many animals, such as giraffes, zebras, and elephants.

Madagascar is an island in the Indian Ocean. It is the world's fourth-largest island. The country of Seychelles is a chain of more than 90 islands.

In the west, the dry savanna gives way to the Kalahari and Namib Deserts. These deserts cover parts of Namibia, Angola, and Botswana.

The Great Zimbabwe

The word *zimbabwe* refers to an important village. Archaeologists believe there were several such villages in Southern Africa, but the Great Zimbabwe is the only one that has survived. This site is very mysterious, and little is known of its history. The Shona people built it before the 1300s. At some point, they began encircling their villages with stone walls. These walls offered privacy and security. They were made of stone slabs held together without any mortar. No one knows why the Great Zimbabwe was abandoned in the 1500s. Today its ruins lie near the city of Masvingo.

Could you survive living in the desert? The San are experts at it. They were the first known humans to live in the harsh Kalahari Desert. Today, only a few follow the traditional ways of life. They speak languages that include clicking sounds. Outsiders find them very hard to pronounce.

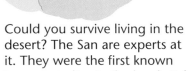

Angola
Population: 10,770,000
Languages: Portuguese, Bantu, Umbundu, other tribal languages
Capital: Luanda
Average person's buying power: $1,600

Botswana
Population: 1,580,000
Languages: English, Setswana
Capital: Gaborone
Average person's buying power: $9,500

Comoros
Population: 640,000
Languages: Arabic, French, Shikomoro
Capital: Moroni
Average person's buying power: $720

Madagascar
Population: 16,980,000
Languages: French, Malagasy
Capital: Antananarivo
Average person's buying power: $760

Malawi
Population: 11,660,000
Languages: English, Chichewa
Capital: Lilongwe
Average person's buying power: $670

Mauritius
Population: 1,220,000
Languages: English, French, Creole, Hindi
Capital: Port Louis
Average person's buying power: $11,000

Mozambique
Population: 17,480,000
Language: Portuguese
Capital: Maputo
Average person's

buying power: $1,000

Namibia
Population: 1,930,000
Languages: Afrikaans, English, German
Capital: Windhoek
Average person's buying power: $6,900

Seychelles
Population: 85,000
Languages: English, French, Creole
Capital: Victoria

Average person's buying power: $7,800

Zambia
Population: 10,310,000
Languages: English, Bemba, Kaonda, Lozi, and more than 70 other local languages
Capital: Lusaka
Average person's buying power: $890

Zimbabwe
Population: 12,580,000
Languages: English, Shona, Sindebele
Capital: Harare
Average person's buying power: $2,400

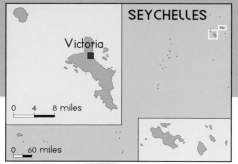

SEYCHELLES

Victoria

0 4 8 miles

0 60 miles

Moroni ■ COMOROS

MALAWI
■ Lilongwe

Zambezi

arare

MOZAMBIQUE

vingo

INDIAN OCEAN

MOZAMBIQUE CHANNEL

MADAGASCAR
■ Antananarivo

■ Maputo

0 60 120 180 240 miles

The Indian Ocean islands of Mauritius and the Seychelles are absolutely beautiful! That's why a main industry here is tourism. The islands' remote location and spectacular beaches have attracted a lot of people. Today there are many hotels and resorts to choose from.

MAURITIUS
Port Louis ■

REUNION
(France)

The Zambezi River once flowed freely through Zambia and Zimbabwe. But these nations were growing, and they needed electric power. So the governments built a dam to supply the areas with hydroelectric power. The dam created one of the largest human-made lakes in history— Lake Kariba.

Madagascar's wildlife is unique! In fact, most of the island's 200,000 plant and animal species live nowhere else in the world. The island's best-known animals are the lemurs, shown here. But you will also find the tenrec, the Malagasy mongoose, the fossa, chameleons, tortoises, moths, and butterflies.

South Africa

South Africa sits on the southern tip of Africa. It is a land of green grasslands, towering mountains, and hot desert. South Africa is also one of the continent's richest countries. For many years, the country was known as "the land of gold and diamonds."

Most of South Africa is covered with flat sections of land called plateaus. Mountains called the Great Escarpment separate the plateau from the coastal regions.

South Africa surrounds two small independent kingdoms. They are home to the Sotho and Swazi peoples. Lesotho is a land of mountains and plateaus. Swaziland is covered with the veld, or grassy plains.

South Africa
Population: 42,770,000
Languages: Afrikaans, English, Ndebele, Sotho, Zulu
Capitals: Pretoria, Cape Town, and Bloemfontein
Average person's buying power: $10,000
Land area: 471,010 square miles
Unit of currency: rand
Major cities: Cape Town, Durban, Johannesburg, Pretoria, Soweto
Industries: mining, automobile assembly, metalworking, machinery, textiles
Agricultural products: corn, wheat, sugarcane, beef, poultry
Lesotho
Population: 1,870,000
Languages: Sesotho, English
Capital: Maseru
Average person's buying power: $2,700
Swaziland
Population: 1,170,000
Languages: English, siSwati
Capitals: Mbabane and Lobamba
Average person's buying power: $4,400

If you explored the veld of South Africa, you'd probably spot a springbok. This antelope lives in these grassy plains. It gets its name because it springs more than ten feet into the air when frightened. It leaps like this to fool its predators, such as lions and cheetahs.

NAMIBIA

ATLANTIC OCEAN

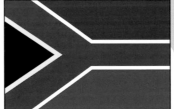

This is the flag of South Africa. The green stripes come together to make one stripe, symbolizing the struggle to overcome apartheid and come together in unity. The other colors symbolize the peoples of South Africa: Africans and Europeans. The flag reminds the people of South Africa to work together.

Cape Town

The Cape of Good Hope is a peninsula stretching from Cape Town at the southeastern corner of the continent. In the past, ships sailing south from Europe looked forward to turning this corner and heading for India. This marks the point where the Atlantic and Indian Oceans mix.

Johannesburg was built on gold. The shiny metal has made Johannesburg the most important industrial and financial center for Africa. Gold mines lie in the earth around the city.

BOTSWANA

ZIMBABWE

MOZAMBIQUE

Pretoria ■
Johannesburg ○ ○
Soweto

SOUTH AFRICA

Mbabane ■
Lobamba ■
SWAZILAND

Bloemfontein ■
Maseru ■
LESOTHO

Durban ○

INDIAN OCEAN

0   60   120   180   240 miles

Under apartheid, blacks and whites were separated from each other. Whites had more rights than blacks. But the people wanted apartheid to change. Two black South Africans helped change it. They are Nelson Mandela and Bishop Desmond Tutu. Apartheid was ended in 1994. In that same year, Mandela became the first black president of South Africa.

Diamond and Gold Mining

Imagine finding a pretty rock, taking it home, and learning it was a diamond! You'd probably go look for more, right? This is what happened to a young boy many years ago in South Africa. Soon after, people flocked to the area. South Africa's diamond business had begun. Today diamonds are still a big business here.

In addition to diamonds, South Africa also has a lot of other minerals. In fact, the country is the world's biggest producer of gold.

Is it any wonder why South Africa earned the name "the land of gold and diamonds"?

Settlers from the Netherlands and England started to come here more than 400 years ago. They took control from African peoples, such as the Zulu, Xhosa, and Sotho. During the 1900s, South Africa's system of government was called apartheid. It separated the races and kept the black Africans from having power.

Australia

Is Australia a country or a continent? It's both! The country of Australia is the world's smallest continent.

Australia's center is covered with a vast, dry desert and grassland known as the Outback. Very few people live in its harsh climate. Most Australians live in or near cities along the eastern and southern coasts. Near the ocean, the weather is warm, and the land is rich for farming. And in the ocean, the Great Barrier Reef, the world's largest living structure, stretches for 1,250 miles.

Before Europeans began to settle here in the late 1700s, Aborigines were the only people on this continent.

Marsupials

Many of Australia's animals are very unusual. You already know about kangaroos and koalas. They are marsupials. Marsupials are a kind of mammal that gives birth to tiny offspring. The mother then carries the baby in a pouch. There are about 250 different kinds of marsupials. Wallabies, wombats, and Tasmanian devils are three more.

Other unusual Australian animals include the platypus and echidna. They are the only mammals that hatch their young from eggs. Australia is home to more than 700 kinds of birds. The best known is the loud kookaburra.

I N D O

Do you think of the boomerang as a toy or a weapon? It can be both. Aborigines would throw these curved pieces of wood as weapons for hunting. Others can be thrown for fun. They return to the thrower.

INDIAN OCEAN

Can you guess what a didgeridoo is? It is a musical instrument! The Aborigines of northern Australia play the didgeridoo in religious ceremonies. It is a long wooden tube. To play it, you blow into the tube, and out comes an eerie, booming sound.

Perth

0   150   300   450 miles

What do you suppose happens at a sheep station? Is it a train station for sheep? Do people come to ride sheep? No. In Australia, sheep and cattle ranches are called stations. Sheep and cattle farming is big business here. In fact, Australia is the world's biggest supplier of wool.

Population: 19,740,000	**Major cities:** Sydney, Melbourne, Brisbane, Perth
Language: English	**Industries:** mining, industrial and transportation equipment, food processing, chemicals, steel
Capital: Canberra	
Average person's buying power: $27,000	
Land area: 2,967,910 square miles	**Agricultural products:** wheat, barley, sugarcane, cattle, sheep
Unit of currency: Australian dollar	

E S I A PAPUA NEW GUINEA

ST TIMOR

SOLOMON
ISLANDS

CORAL
SEA

Great Barrier Reef

AUSTRALIA

▲
Uluru
(Ayers Rock)

○ Brisbane

SOUTHERN
OCEAN

○ Sydney

■ Canberra

Melbourne

Tasmania

Does this building look like the giant sails of a ship? It's supposed to. That's what the builder wanted it to look like. This is the Sydney Opera House. Sydney is Australia's oldest city. The Opera House sits beside the harbor. Built in 1973, it has become Australia's most familiar landmark.

Uluru is the Aborigines' name for Ayers Rock. This ancient block of sandstone sits in Australia's Northern Territory. It is the world's largest monolith, or single block of rock. It is sacred to the native people. Aboriginal paintings decorate the cave walls. In 1985, Uluru was returned to the Aborigines.

Melbourne is Australia's second-largest city. It is a busy seaport and Australia's main financial city. Downtown Melbourne is on the northern shore of Port Phillip Bay. Historic buildings sit side by side with modern architecture, creating a unique and beautiful skyline.

Pacific Islands

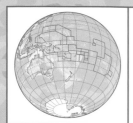

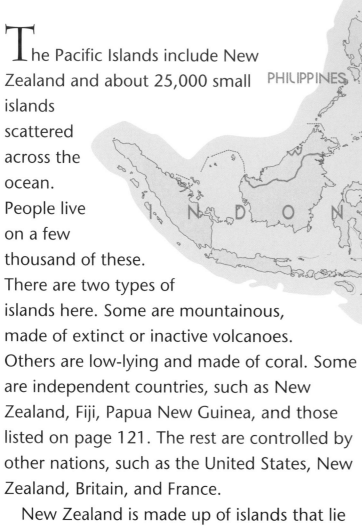

The Pacific Islands include New Zealand and about 25,000 small islands scattered across the ocean. People live on a few thousand of these. There are two types of islands here. Some are mountainous, made of extinct or inactive volcanoes. Others are low-lying and made of coral. Some are independent countries, such as New Zealand, Fiji, Papua New Guinea, and those listed on page 121. The rest are controlled by other nations, such as the United States, New Zealand, Britain, and France.

New Zealand is made up of islands that lie more than 1,000 miles southeast of Australia. Most New Zealanders live on the two main islands, North Island and South Island.

Rugby football is New Zealand's national sport. It is a relative of American football. There are many local rugby teams in New Zealand. These teams might be made up of men or women. Almost everybody in New Zealand enjoys playing rugby.

Cricket is almost as popular as rugby in New Zealand. New Zealand has a national cricket team. You can often see people playing neighborhood cricket games, as well.

Island Dress and Dances

The peoples of the Pacific Islands are as different as the islands they call home. But they have at least one thing in common: Their traditional customs are an important part of their everyday lives.

In Papua New Guinea, tribes hold festivals of dancing, singing, and feasting called sing-sings. Tribe members decorate their bodies and faces with paint. They wear fancy masks and headdresses. The Maori people of New Zealand perform dances called action songs. Long ago, it was common for men and women to wear tattoos on their faces. Today, they reenact this tradition by painting similar designs on their faces.

The Pacific Islands are not all the same. Some, like those shown here, are high islands, made of hills and even mountains. Others are low islands. Most of the low islands are atolls. An atoll is a coral reef that surrounds a lagoon. Most of the low islands barely peek above the water.

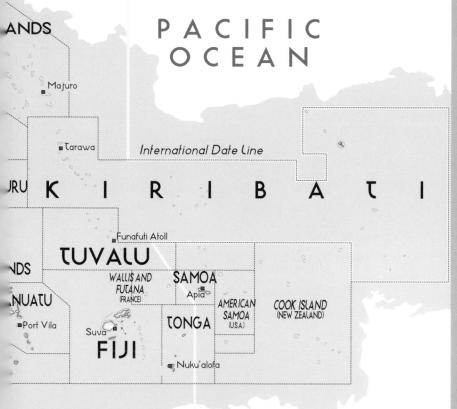

PACIFIC OCEAN

International Date Line

ANDS
Majuro

JRU K I R I B A T I

Tarawa

NDS TUVALU

NUATU

Port Vila

WALLIS AND FUTANA (FRANCE)

SAMOA
Apia

Funafuti Atoll

Suva TONGA

FIJI

Nuku'alofa

AMERICAN SAMOA (U.S.A.)

COOK ISLAND (NEW ZEALAND)

If you look at a hillside in New Zealand from a distance, you might think you see a cotton field. But look closer. That's not cotton on the hillside. Those are sheep! Sheep are big business in New Zealand. These animals are raised for both meat and wool.

Fiji
Population: 870,000
Languages: English, Fijian, Hindustani
Capital: Suva
Average person's buying power: $5,500

Kiribati
Population: 100,000
Languages: I-Kiribati, English
Capital: Tarawa
Average person's buying power: $840

Marshall Islands
Population: 60,000
Languages: English, Marshallese
Capital: Majuro
Average person's buying power: $1,600

Micronesia
Population: 110,000
Languages: English, Trukese, Pohnpeian, Yapese
Capital: Palikir
Average person's buying power: $2,000

Nauru
Population: 13,000
Languages: Nauruan, English
Capital: no official capital
Average person's buying power: $5,000

New Zealand
Population: 3,960,000
Languages: English, Maori
Capital: Wellington
Average person's buying power: $20,200

Palau
Population: 20,000
Languages: English, Palauan
Capital: Koror
Average person's buying power: $9,000

Papua New Guinea
Population: 5,300,000
Languages: Motu, 750 local languages
Capital: Port Moresby
Average person's buying power: $2,300

Samoa
Population: 180,000
Languages: Samoan, English
Capital: Apia
Average person's buying power: $5,600

Solomon Islands
Population: 510,000
Language: Melanesian
Capital: Honiara
Average person's buying power: $1,700

Tonga
Population: 110,000
Languages: Tongan, English
Capital: Nuku'alofa
Average person's buying power: $2,200

Tuvalu
Population: 12,000
Languages: Tuvaluan, English, Samoan
Capital: Funafuti
Average person's buying power: $1,100

Vanuatu
Population: 200,000
Languages: English, French, Bislama, more than 100 local languages
Capital: Port Vila
Average person's buying power: $2,900

Wellington

Mt. Cook

NEW ZEALAND

The Maoris call New Zealand's highest peak Aoraki, which means "cloud piercer." It is also known as Mount Cook. It is part of the Southern Alps, a mountain range that covers much of South Island. Mount Cook and its surrounding area offer some of New Zealand's most spectacular scenery and skiing.

Polar Regions

SOUTH AMERICA

WEDDELL SEA

Cape Horn

BELLINGSHAUSEN SEA

AMUNDSEN SEA

Only one word describes the Polar Regions—cold! They surround the North and South Poles. These barren places are covered in ice and snow all year.

The Arctic is the area around the North Pole. It is made up of a large ocean—the Arctic Ocean— almost completely surrounded by land. The frozen continent of Antarctica, covered by a giant ice cap, surrounds the South Pole. Its mountains and valleys are below the ice.

Earth is a giant magnet! Its poles are the north magnetic pole and the south magnetic pole. They are near the North and South Poles but are different. Because earth's magnetic field changes, the magnetic poles move. A compass needle points toward the north magnetic pole.

Yes, animals live in Antarctica! But they do not roam the land. Instead they live in and above its surrounding waters. They include penguins, seals, and whales. They have a layer of fat that keeps them warm in the cold. Whales eat a tiny creature like shrimp known as a krill.

Ice, Ice, and More Ice

If you are looking for ice, the Polar Regions offer all kinds. A huge ice sheet covers Antarctica. It is more than two miles thick in some places. Along the coast, the ice sheet hangs over the ocean, forming huge ice shelves.

Icebergs are found in both the Arctic and Antarctica. They are large chunks of ice that break off from ice sheets or glaciers that meet the sea. Some can be as big as small countries! The icebergs float off into the ocean. If they float into warmer waters, they can be a danger to ships.

About 100 years ago, the poles were the last places on earth yet to be reached. The race was on! Traveling by dogsled, Norwegian Roald Amundsen reached the South Pole in 1911. The first to reach the North Pole alone was Japanese explorer Naomi Uemura in 1978. He, too, traveled by dogsled.

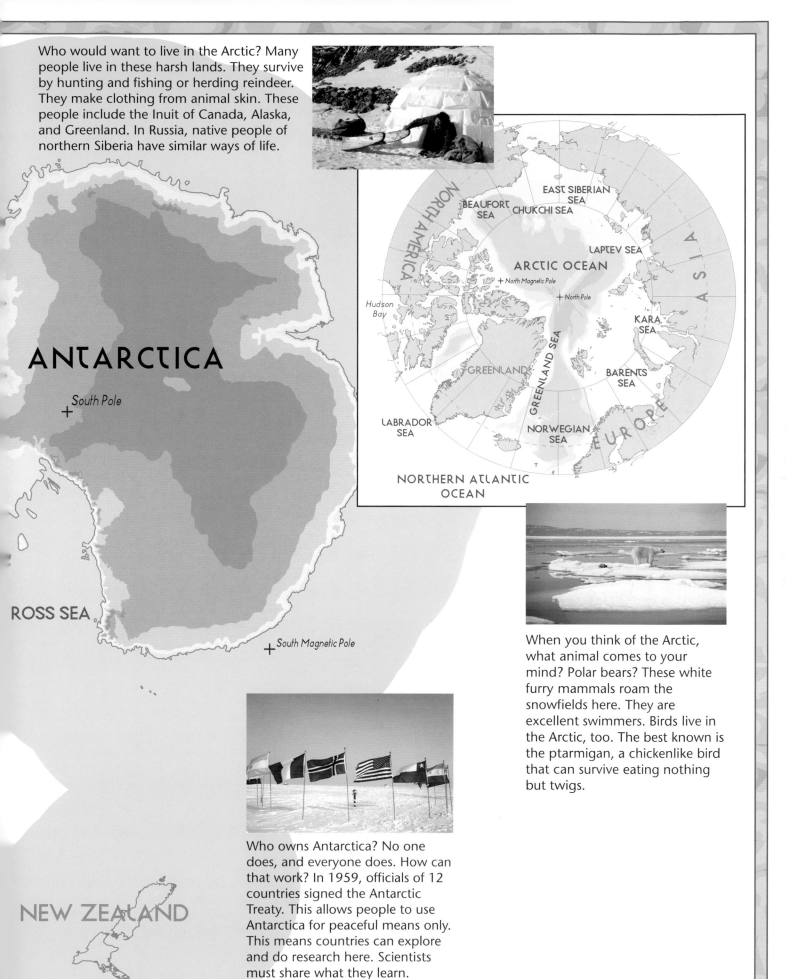

Who would want to live in the Arctic? Many people live in these harsh lands. They survive by hunting and fishing or herding reindeer. They make clothing from animal skin. These people include the Inuit of Canada, Alaska, and Greenland. In Russia, native people of northern Siberia have similar ways of life.

ANTARCTICA

South Pole
+

ROSS SEA

+ South Magnetic Pole

NEW ZEALAND

NORTH AMERICA

BEAUFORT SEA
CHUKCHI SEA
EAST SIBERIAN SEA
LAPTEV SEA

ARCTIC OCEAN

+ North Magnetic Pole
+ North Pole

Hudson Bay

KARA SEA

GREENLAND

GREENLAND SEA

BARENTS SEA

ASIA

LABRADOR SEA

NORWEGIAN SEA

EUROPE

NORTHERN ATLANTIC OCEAN

When you think of the Arctic, what animal comes to your mind? Polar bears? These white furry mammals roam the snowfields here. They are excellent swimmers. Birds live in the Arctic, too. The best known is the ptarmigan, a chickenlike bird that can survive eating nothing but twigs.

Who owns Antarctica? No one does, and everyone does. How can that work? In 1959, officials of 12 countries signed the Antarctic Treaty. This allows people to use Antarctica for peaceful means only. This means countries can explore and do research here. Scientists must share what they learn.

 Afghanistan
 Albania
 Algeria
 Andorra
 Angola
 Antigua and Barbuda

 Argentina
 Armenia
 Australia
 Austria
 Azerbaijan
 The Bahamas

 Bahrain
 Bangladesh
 Barbados
 Belarus
 Belgium
 Belize

 Benin
 Bhutan
 Bolivia
 Bosnia and Herzegovina
 Botswana
 Brazil

 Brunei
 Bulgaria
 Burkina Faso
 Burundi
 Cambodia
 Cameroon

 Canada
 Cape Verde
 Central African Republic
 Chad
 Chile
 China

 Colombia
 Comoros
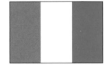 Costa Rica
 Côte d'Ivoire
 Croatia
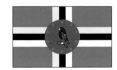 Cuba

 Cyprus
 Czech Republic
 Democratic Republic of the Congo
 Denmark
 Djibouti
 Dominica

 Dominican Republic

 East Timor

 Ecuador

 Egypt

 El Salvador

 Equatorial Guinea

 Eritrea

 Estonia

 Ethiopia

 Fiji

 Finland

 France

 Gabon

 The Gambia

 Georgia

 Germany

 Ghana

 Greece

 Grenada

 Guatemala

 Guinea

 Guinea-Bissau

 Guyana

 Haiti

 Holy See (Vatican City)

 Honduras

 Hungary

 Iceland

 India

 Indonesia

 Iran

 Iraq

 Ireland

 Israel

 Italy

 Jamaica

 Japan

 Jordan

 Kazakhstan

 Kenya

 Kiribati

 Kuwait

 Kyrgyzstan

 Laos

 Latvia

 Lebanon

 Lesotho

 Liberia

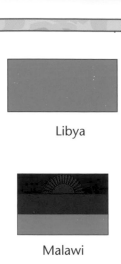 Libya

 Liechtenstein

 Lithuania

 Luxembourg

 Macedonia

Madagascar

 Malawi

 Malaysia

 Maldives

 Mali

 Malta

Marshall Islands

 Mauritania

 Mauritius

 Mexico

 Micronesia

 Moldova

 Monaco

 Mongolia

 Morocco

 Mozambique

 Myanmar

 Namibia

Nauru

 Nepal

 Netherlands

 New Zealand

 Nicaragua

 Niger

Nigeria

 North Korea

 Norway

 Oman

 Pakistan

 Palau

 Panama

 Papua New Guinea

 Paraguay

 Peru

 Philippines

Poland

 Portugal

 Qatar

 Republic of the Congo

 Romania

 Russian Federation

 Rwanda

 Saint Kitts and Nevis

 Saint Lucia

 Saint Vincent and Grenadines

 Samoa

 San Marino

 São Tomé and Principe

 Saudi Arabia

 Senegal

 Serbia and Montenegro

 Seychelles

 Sierra Leone

 Singapore

 Slovakia

 Slovenia

 Solomon Islands

 Somalia

 South Africa

 South Korea

 Spain

 Sri Lanka

 Sudan

 Suriname

 Swaziland

 Sweden

 Switzerland

 Syria

 Taiwan

 Tajikistan

 Tanzania

 Thailand

 Togo

 Tonga

 Trinidad and Tobago

 Tunisia

 Turkey

 Turkmenistan

 Tuvalu

 Uganda

 Ukraine

 United Arab Emirates

 United Kingdom

 United States

Uruguay

 Uzbekistan

 Vanuatu

 Venezuela

Vietnam

Yemen

 Zambia

 Zimbabwe

127

Index